PRENTICE HALL
professional educator's library

HOW•TO MANAGE INSTRUCTION IN THE BLOCK

Douglas S. Fleming
Barbara A. Fleming

About the Authors

Doug and Barbara Fleming provide schools and districts with information, assistance, and training in team building, group problem solving, and school planning. They also work with organizations and associations that support teacher leadership. Their current workshops include teaching in a block schedule, school-based decision making, interdisciplinary curriculum, and multiple assessment procedures. They each conduct peer coaching and mentor training programs.

Doug and Barbara have designed, conducted, and evaluated seminars, conferences, and train-the-trainer programs throughout the United States. The National Education Association, The American Library Association, and the Appalachia Educational Laboratory are examples of organizations that have contracted with them as writers, researchers, and consultants.

Doug is co-moderator of the Internet-based discussion list iti@ael.org—an on-line forum for exchanging practices in interdisciplinary teamed instruction. Both Doug and Barbara welcome questions and suggestions from readers of this book. You can contact them at the e-mail address: dfleming@tiac.net.

Acknowledgments

We would like to thank the following for the use of their materials:

Gary Kinsey, Clovis West High School, Fresno, CA
Bena Kallick, Education Consultant, Westport, CT
Cerylle C. Moffett, Education Consultant, Alexandria, VA

Design and Page Composition: Siren design, Inc.
Cover Design: Suzanne Schineller
Cover Photo: Rick Iwasaki/Tony Stone Images

Printed in the United States of America.
ISBN: 0-13-434441-3

3 4 5 6 7 8 9 10   02 01 00 99 98

Table of Contents

INTRODUCTION

—More than 40 percent of high schools nationwide are using some form of block or alternative scheduling (1996).

—By 2010, as many as 75 percent of schools will be using alternative schedules.

—Currently, the 4x4 schedule is the most popular and successful.

—The alternating day (A/B) is the second most highly used schedule.

WHY CHANGE SCHEDULES?

There is a great deal of interest in block scheduling now at the high school level. Middle schools have been using some form of flexible scheduling for years, but why the interest in block scheduling in high school? Many of the same reasons apply across the grades. Some of the reasons for moving to a block schedule are:

- To increase the time that students spend in quality learning situations.
- To encourage the use of a variety of instructional models.
- To provide for more in-depth exploration of a topic.
- To improve school climate and decrease stress on teachers and students.
- To reduce discipline problems.
- To accommodate different learning needs.
- To focus on fewer subjects at one time.

What are some of the benefits of having extended opportunities for classwork? According to *A Guide to Authentic Instruction and Assessment* published by the Wisconsin Center for Education Research, the benefits range from providing students with opportunities to broaden their higher order thinking skills by manipulating information and ideas to having students demonstrate their knowledge and understanding of concepts and content through alternative assessment. Along the way among other benefits, students engage in substantive conversations with one another and with their teachers and learn valuable research and organizational skills.

A SHIFT IN EMPHASIS

Block scheduling requires a shift in emphasis in the teaching and learning process.

From	To
What the teacher does	What the student can do
Teaching as telling	Learning as doing
Covering the content	Understanding important ideas
Mastery of facts and skills in isolation	Tasks that call for problem solving, critical thinking, and creativity
Absorbing knowledge	Producing and using knowledge
Expecting students to think	Requiring students to show their thinking

These changes in expectations for both the teacher and the student require that teachers use strategies that create an active learning environment in the classroom and that students take responsibility for their own learning. A classroom making the best use of the extended time periods will see students engaged in dialogues among themselves and with the teacher, working on problem-based and project-based learning, using authentic tasks to demonstrate competence and to self-assess, and involved in cooperative learning and work stations. *How to Manage Instruction in the Block* will help you, the teacher, by providing you with a variety of teaching and learning strategies to maximize the intent of block scheduling—making the most effective use of time to help students achieve.

THE AUDIENCE FOR THIS BOOK

The primary audience for this book is classroom teachers (and administrators) who are considering, planning, or already implementing a block-of-time schedule in their school. For some of you, the ideas in *How to Manage Instruction in the Block* will serve as helpful reminders of good practices that you may not have used for a while. The contents will expand upon your teaching repertoires. For others of you, the ideas in this book will be new, and the contents will provide helpful descriptions, guidelines, and pointers to more effective ways of organizing time and space in your classrooms. For still others, the ideas will validate your classroom choices, judgments, and organizing strategies.

A secondary audience for *How to Manage Instruction in the Block* is central office administrators, curriculum coordinators, assessment specialists, and staff developers. The concrete illustrations of classroom management and teaching practices may represent a useful resource for planning professional development programs; for mentoring, coaching, and supervising classroom teachers; and for facilitating the work of district- and school-level planning committees.

HOW THIS BOOK IS ORGANIZED

How to Manage Instruction in the Block is organized into seven chapters and an Appendices. The first two chapters establish a foundation for working in a block-of- time schedule—how teachers can get classrooms ready for block-of-time learning, and how teachers can adapt or adjust curriculum materials for use in block-of-time schedules. Chapters 3 through 6 illustrate a range of appropriate practices for teaching in a block-of-time schedule—interactive strategies to promote higher-order thinking, problem solving, communication, and teamwork. The final chapter provides answers to frequently asked questions encountered in professional development sessions on block scheduling. The Appendices provide a checklist of action steps for teaching in the block and one for assessing small group work.

WAYS TO USE THIS BOOK

If you are a classroom teacher, you may be most interested in the chapters on managing classroom routines, organizing small group learning, or designing lessons for extended periods of learning. The sample lesson plans illustrate ways to use time in block schedules. A lesson planning template is provided so that you can reproduce and use it as a guide for your own lessons. A lesson design rubric has also been included for self-assessment.

If you are a teacher leader or staff developer, you may be more interested in the chapters on "short takes" and blocking lessons, because these chapters lend themselves to faculty discussion, enactment, and modeling. Each of the chapters emphasizes the use of appropriate pacing, variety, and engagement so necessary to successful learning.

Administrators and planning team members may find the chapters on making plans and checking progress and responses to frequently asked questions as well as the list of selected resources especially helpful.

By using the step-by-step format presented in *How to Manage Instruction in the Block,* you can make the best use of a block-of-time schedule to create an active learning environment so your students can achieve success. So good luck, and let us know your success stories!

Douglas S. Fleming   Barbara A. Fleming

MANAGING CLASSROOM ROUTINES IN BLOCK-OF-TIME SCHEDULES

CHAPTER 1

A block-scheduled classroom creates an opportunity to provide students with practical experiences using skills that are a bridge to the real world of jobs and adult responsibilities. Those experiences go beyond memorization into a world of reasoning, and beyond lecture followed by drill and practice to active coaching by the teacher and authentic problem-solving by the student.

WHAT STUDENTS ARE DOING

Students in a block-scheduled classroom are interacting with one another as well as working independently just as adults do. Textbooks are just one of many learning resources. Students are working with materials such as hammers, staplers, and scales and technologies such as calculators and computers as information processing, problem-solving, and communication tools. They are applying their skills to real-life problems, not just practicing skills in isolation from a more complex context. Ample time is allowed for solving these complex problems. Students find that there is not necessarily a single solution, but arrive at what they consider to be the best solution and are able to explain the different ways they have achieved their results and are able to defend one choice over another. Students in an active learning environment, which is the best of what block-scheduled classrooms offer, communicate ideas through writing, oral demonstrations, models, drawing, and logical argumentation.

Teams or cooperative groups work together to help one another learn to challenge and defend possible solutions. They design and carry out research using library media centers, com-

**Related Practices
and Policies:
A Keyword Checklist
for Internet Searching**

case-study method

cooperative-group
  learning

critical-thinking skills

graphic organizers

integration of
  technology

interdisciplinary
  curriculum

multiple intelligences

performance assessment

problem-based learning

process education

project-based learning

senior projects

teamed instruction

thematic units

socratic questioning

student-centered

munity resources, the Internet, a variety of laboratory experiments, and original sources. They engage in intensive project work focused on themes that culminate in exhibitions or presentations: dramatic reenactments, debates, or performances.

WHAT TEACHERS ARE DOING

Teachers are guides who assist students in exploring multiple solutions and interpretations and challenge students to think deeply. Teachers in an active learning environment are moving around the room to keep everyone engaged in productive work and finding ways to have one-to-one interactions with students. Listeners and observers, teachers are conferencing and assessing more than presenting material. Their subject matter is not only discipline specific but includes teaching and coaching for better organization, information use, and time management.

Teachers are encouraging students to raise and discuss questions for which there are no textbook or "one right" answer. They are providing access to resources and helping students make appropriate use of technology, media, and other tools to represent their understandings of concepts and to test hypotheses. Teachers are promoting student use of inquiry and creativity by encouraging the statement of new problems that are variations or extensions of given situations. They are designing investigations that explore practical applications of theories and concepts.

Working together, teachers of different subject areas are making connections between and among disciplines to show how what students are learning in one area is a part of another subject(s) that students are studying. Using assessment approaches that measure problem solving and understanding, teachers evaluate more than just memory and speed. They are requiring their students to demonstrate knowledge and skills through products and performances.

PUTTING MANAGEMENT IN PLACE

Block-of-time scheduling allows both teachers and students to explore topics and develop new skills in more depth and with more practical application of competencies than in traditionally scheduled classes. You will find that the longer periods promote more small group work, more research projects, more presentations, authentic assessment, and so on—active learning. The skills and competencies that students will develop are the ones that they will need in the workplace.

Students rarely come to class with these competencies fully developed or "preinstalled." One of the important characteristics of a block-scheduled classroom is the ability to help students develop these skills and competencies. As a teacher, you will undoubtedly need to prepare your students to function in the block-scheduled environment.

In order to do this, you first need to prepare yourself to work in a block-scheduled organization. The climate of the class will have to undergo a change as well as classroom routines and procedures. You will need to communicate to your students the change in expectations that comes with a different teaching and learning environment. To achieve your curriculum requirements in the midst of these changes will require that you learn some new time management skills as well.

The suggestions on the following pages will help you with each of these steps as you prepare to work within a block schedule.

See Appendix A, "Checklist of Action Steps for Teaching in a Block-Scheduled Classroom," to help you put into the practice the tips and tools in this chapter.

Step 1: Preparing Yourself

You as the teacher need to maintain your own focus and energy during extended periods of learning. This step provides suggestions to help you start your year on the right track and to maintain that momentum.

1. Develop lesson plans for the first two weeks of school. Lesson plans provide the "mental rehearsal" needed to adapt to the flow of a block-of-time schedule. They also help identify materials, supplies, and other resources needed for your activities.

2. Develop a pacing guide for your course. This will help keep you on target with major curriculum goals and expectations (see page 31).

3. Develop a Calendar of Assignments and Activities. A calendar keeps both teacher and students on track. Distribute the calendar to students every two weeks.

4. Post a Daily Agenda. Use the board or an overhead projector so that everyone can refer to it. It's all right to modify it when needed, but using this technique helps keep both you and your students aware of how time is being used, and what tasks still need to be done.

5. Use Your Curriculum Standards. Your state and district curriculum standards and the national standards for your discipline are helpful tools for planning lessons. Use classroom time to make sure that students can demonstrate them.

6. Materials and Supplies. Have the materials and supplies you need for each lesson available and ready to be distributed.

What I need to do to prepare myself for the block-of-time schedule:

_____

_____

_____

_____

_____

_____

_____

_____

_____

Step 2: Preparing the Climate

This section suggests things you can do to maintain a classroom that signals orderliness, responsibility, and seriousness of purpose.

1. Establish a climate of work in the classroom. Post a chart titled "What to Do If You Finish Early," which gives students concrete suggestions for using the rest of their time if they finish an activity early.

2. Show that student questioning, investigation, and ownership are welcomed. Post a "Question of the Day" and allow teams to propose a solution in a sealed envelope.

3. Establish a climate of respect for self and property. Assign a day for each student to clean his/her desk regularly.

What I need to do to prepare students for a climate of work in my classroom:

_____

_____

_____

_____

_____

_____

_____

_____

_____

_____

_____

_____

_____

_____

_____

_____

_____

Step 3: Preparing Classroom Routines and Procedures

Modifying classroom routines and procedures for the longer periods of instructional time in block-scheduled classrooms can ease the transition to working in longer periods of time for both you and your students.

1. Arrange tables and chairs or desks in a way that signals that students will be working in groups and at learning stations.

2. Develop a seating chart for the new room arrangement.

3. Set up a file folder for each student as needed.

4. Develop a "routine" for attendance, small group work, etc., that could be executed by students and a substitute teacher in your absence.

5. Set up different times during the period for taking attendance, reporting announcements, issuing corridor passes, returning homework assignments, providing bathroom breaks, etc.

6. Construct a chart listing student job assignments.

7. Create or select a form that can be attached to student work for parent/guardian signature and comments.

8. Establish and explain specific rules for classroom areas. You might set up a folder or booklet for these rules where students can look them up if they forget what is appropriate behavior for the classroom.

- Doors
- Windows
- Student desks/work areas/learning stations
- Wall space
- Bookcases

- Teacher desk/work area
- Teaching/learning materials
- Teaching/learning equipment
- General classroom supplies
- Special materials
- Emergency/first aid

What I need to do to prepare my classroom routines and procedures:

_____

_____

_____

Step 4: Preparing the Students

Students are often the overlooked factor in planning for learning in a block-of-time schedule. It is essential that you communicate to them the change in expectations that will occur with more project-based and problem-based learning, and help them become capable and responsible managers of their own learning. This will require teaching and coaching organizational, communication, and time management skills.

1. Use self-assessment tools, quizzes, and checklists to prompt students to think about what they themselves can do to improve their learning.

2. As you assign projects, provide specific strategies for organizing, ordering, or displaying information.

3. Use posters, graphics, overhead transparencies, artwork, time management tips and testimonials from other students, quotations, and useful reminders to help students organize their time.

4. Teach general study skills such as taking notes, citing references, preparing reports, preparing class presentations, and using computers to locate and access information.

5. Teach students to use word webs, mind maps, and other graphic organizers.

6. Introduce, model, and explain a range of practical study tools, including:
   • Providing quiet study areas, without distractions
   • SQ3R method (Survey, Question, Read, Review, Recite)
   • Active reading strategies
   • Mnemonic devices, word association, rhythm, visualization
   • Study groups
   • Goal setting
   • Time management
   • Dealing with test anxiety
   • Problem-solving models

7. Devise a checklist for studying or reading text materials in your specific discipline.

8. Make up note-taking guidelines for discussion groups or lectures, listing general categories of what students should be listening for and taking notes about.

9. Provide students with outlines and timelines for planning a team research project in your discipline.

10. Develop rating scales for student-generated written reports, oral presentations, and other learning products.

11. Share guidelines for effective student writing in your subject area.

12. Post tips for sharing a single computer, reference manual, or other items to be used by students working in teams in your class.

13. Conduct special coaching sessions for students on meeting the challenge of writing responses to open-ended questions on standardized tests, developing essays, or preparing laboratory reports and research papers.

14. Require that students keep a notebook and provide them with a notebook self-evaluation checklist to ensure that all information is up to date.

15. Once a week, contact parents of students with "D" or "F" grades. With a block-of-time schedule, it is critical to "stay on top" of students who are slipping behind.

16. Share expectations with students about length of time for tests. Students who are accustomed to a having a test take a full class period may assume that the same is true in a block-of time-schedule. A block schedule does NOT mean that tests will use the entire period.

17. Help students make wise course selections, with a balance of academic and nonacademic courses. Some students may be tempted to "go heavy" or "go light."

What I can do to prepare students to work in a block-of-time schedule:

_____

_____

_____

_____

_____

_____

_____

_____

Step 5: Managing Instructional Time

Block-of-time schedules often mean that, in total, there are fewer instructional minutes in a course. Good instructional and time management techniques, therefore, ensure that you will be able to provide adequate content coverage in your discipline or subject area.

Beginning Minutes

The first five minutes and the last five minutes of an instructional period are most likely to be remembered. Roll should be taken quickly, and with a minimum of disruption to make the most of this time. Here are some suggestions for taking attendance.

Practical Tip: Have a "Problem of the Day" posted on the board or overhead. Students begin work as soon as they are seated, and you can see at a glance who is missing.

Practical Tip: Have students sit by teams, so you can quickly see who is absent.

Practical Tip: Have folders in a box by the door. As students come in, they take their folder. Collect the remaining folders to determine who is absent.

To check comprehension of the previous session's material and/or to check the homework assignment, consider these tips.

Practical Tip: Have students place tally marks on a chart indicating which problem or question from the previous day's homework they would like to see worked or discussed.

Practical Tip: Each day, draw a "Luck of the Draw" student to summarize what happened in class the day before.

Practical Tip: Select a problem or question similar to one from the previous assignment. Have students solve or answer it without referring to their homework. This gives a quick check on whether they can do it without additional help.

Practical Tip: Put homework answers on an overhead transparency. Students check their work while you walk around the room observing who has or has not completed the assignment. Students put their score at the top of the paper. Walking the room a second time, you can quickly determine if additional review or practice is needed.

Other ideas I have to make effective use of the first few minutes of class:

_____

_____

_____

_____

_____

Avoiding Downtime

Anticipating what needs to be done and what materials are needed so they are available, and coaching students to use various routines that you have chosen will help make the most of instructional time. These strategies help avoid nonproductive "downtime."

Practical Tip: Have a signal, such as an up-raised arm, to alert students quickly for the need for "quiet."

Practical Tip: Designate a specific location for homework and other assignments to be turned in.

Practical Tip: Have all materials, supplies, and other resources for particular activities ready for students as they need them. Designate a specific area where resources are located, and have one team member come to get them as needed.

Practical Tip: Expect students to work in groups and become responsible managers and assessors of their own work and the work of the group.

Practical Tip: Give *visual* as well as verbal directions for transitions and activities. Use an overhead so students can "see" what they need to do.

Other ideas I have for avoiding downtime:

_____

_____

_____

_____

Preparing Your Students for Group Work

Many students do not have experience working in groups and may not be well prepared to function as part of a team. Coaching students for group work may involve a high investment of time initially but will yield high dividends in effective group work and efficient time management.

Practical Tip: Teach, model, and have students practice communication, teamwork, and social skills that are needed for working in groups.

Practical Tip: Teach, model, and have students practice what is expected during group work. Develop together with your students the norms for team work.

Practical Tip: Assign group roles such as recorder, facilitator, etc., to reinforce the work of teams.

Practical Tip: Have each student evaluate his/her own contribution to working in the group and how well the group functioned as a whole.

Practical Tip: Have each student evaluate his/her own contribution to the end product of the group, as well as evaluate the end product itself.

Other ideas I have for preparing my students to work in groups:

_____

_____

_____

_____

_____

Establish Expectations for What Groups Will Do

A set of routines and practice in using them can help you and your students make the most of instructional time. Clear expectations about the routines—clearly communicated to students—is an essential part of this step.

Practical Tip: One person from each team collects homework papers and puts them in a designated location.

Practical Tip: One person from each team gets materials and supplies when needed for a class activity.

Practical Tip: Each team is responsible for maintaining a notebook containing homework assignments, tests/quizzes missed, and a summary of class activities for absent students.

Practical Tip: Teammates seek help from one another on a project before turning to you for assistance.

The routines I need to establish for my students:

_____

_____

_____

_____

10-2

After ten minutes of instruction, students need two minutes to process the information. Processing and reflecting on "received" information increases comprehension and retention.

Practical Tip: Use a "Quick Write" or "Turn to Your Neighbor and . . ." to give students an opportunity to reflect on what has been said (page 37).

Other processing and reflecting devices I can use:

_____

_____

_____

_____

_____

37-90

After 37 minutes of work on a lesson, students need at least 90 seconds in order to stretch and move around. Research shows that this kind of movement actually INCREASES the retention of information being learned.

Practical Tip: Use an energizer such as "Four Corners" or "Round-the-Clock Learning Buddies" to get students up and moving (pages 52 and 59).

Other ideas I have for building in movement:

_____

_____

_____

_____

_____

Transitions

A smooth, orderly flow from one activity to another reduces the likelihood of behavior problems and increases student work involvement.

Practical Tip: While moving from one activity or segment of the lesson to another, use one of the "Short Takes" to keep the momentum going (see Chapter 3).

Transitions I can use include:

_____

_____

_____

_____

_____

Assigning Homework

In many classrooms, homework is a last-minute thing assigned as the bell is ringing. Students, gathering their belongings, are often interested in something other than what the teacher is saying. To avoid any confusion about what is expected, homework should be assigned quickly, in ways that maximize clarity, and at a time when there are no distractions.

Practical Tip: Homework assignments can be posted on the board or class agenda. This makes the directions clear, and allows you to make the last few minutes of class count for learning.

Other ideas I have for posting assignments:

_____

_____

_____

_____

_____

Ending Minutes

Use the last few minutes of the class to emphasis the key points you want students to remember, or have students practice or reflect on the information you want to reinforce.

Practical Tip: Give more practice. Use a "Short Take" such as "Drill Partners" or "Pairs Check" to drill or practice new information (see pages 49 and 54).

Practical Tip: Review. Use an interactive strategy such as "Note to a Friend" to provide a written review of material covered (see page 40).

Practical Tip: Look ahead. Use an activity such as "3-2-1" to collect questions that students may still have about the topic covered (see page 38).

Practical Tip: Challenge. Provide a challenge question using "Turn to Your Neighbor . . ." or similar technique and have students discuss it (see page 37).

Other ideas I have that will use the last few minutes of the class period productively:

_____

_____

_____

_____

_____

ADAPTING YOUR CURRICULUM TO BLOCK-OF-TIME SCHEDULING

You have prepared yourself, the physical environment of your classroom, the climate of your classroom, and your students for a block schedule. You have looked at different routines and strategies for carrying out those routines in a block-scheduled organization. Now what about the curriculum?

This chapter will help you adapt your curriculum to your new time schedule and at the same time help you meet the new interest in standards-based education. The chapter also describes way to compact the curriculum and to integrate broad themes in your teaching to make teaching and learning more project- and problem-based. The final section provides a Pacing Guide to help you put all these pieces together to ensure that what needs to be taught and learned is indeed covered.

MAKING YOUR CURRICULUM STANDARDS-BASED

Many states are developing curriculum frameworks for districts to use in reviewing, refining, or redesigning their existing educational programs. National professional associations such as the National Council of Teachers of Mathematics have taken the lead in refining the essential knowledge, skills, and attitudes that they believe students need to know to succeed in their respective disciplines. These activities have generated much talk and many headlines about standards—sometimes so much talk that the purpose for standards is lost: Curriculum standards tell teachers, students, parents, and the public what our students should be able to know and do.

To ensure that students can meet these expectations, certain givens need to be in place:

- Activities and materials are selected on their capacity to help students learn and apply the curriculum standards.
- Assessment is based on criteria that are directly related to the standards.
- Communication with students, parents, and other teachers about student progress is based on using the same standards for all students.
- All students have opportunities to meet the same standards.
- Assessments are used to determine how well the standards are being met.

We have broken the process of review and redesign of the curriculum into 5 steps to help you ensure that your curriculum content is current and meets the challenges of the 21st century.

Step 1: Reviewing Your Content Standards

Read, discuss, and define for yourself what the "new standards" in your content area should be.

What do your state and district standards require? What does your national professional organization describe as its content standards? How do the three sets work together in practical terms?

See Appendix A, "Checklist of Action Steps for Teaching in a Block-Scheduled Classroom," to help you put into the practice the tips and tools in this chapter.

In science, for example, the national standards state that a good curriculum provides more than just an exposure to a broad range of "domain" or factual knowledge. Standards for an effective science curriculum include the ability to demonstrate inquiry skills (observation, measurement, experimentation), experience in design and technology problem-solving situations, and an understanding of the impact of science and technology on human affairs. How does this correlate to your state's and district's standards?

Step 2: Defining Core Learning Experiences and Situations

With these standards in mind, map backward from the standards you have listed to identify the core learning experiences and situations in which students will have the opportunity to achieve, practice, and demonstrate learning goals.

A sample, generalized map is provided on page 21 to assist you in this identification process. It may not fit all subjects or courses and must be tailored to individual settings, but it will provide a framework to get you started.

MAPPING YOUR STANDARDS-BASED CURRICULUM

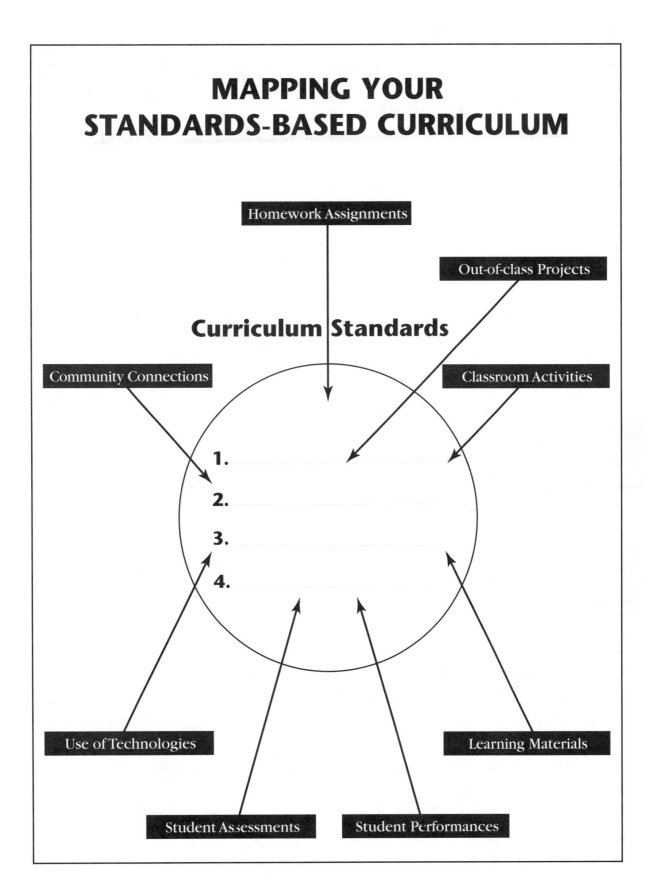

Step 3: Identifying Ways to Achieve the Standards

Systematically identify how the core learning experiences will thread, embed, and reinforce the attainment of the standards.

Your next step after having filled in the learning experiences map is to identify the ways these experiences thread through and embed into the curriculum the content of the standards and reinforce them so that students will be achieving the standards as they work and learn in your class. The following questions ask you to identify how your classroom practices can be adapted to ensure that the standards are being met.

• Do my homework assignments promote attainment of curriculum standards? How?

_____

_____

_____

• Do out-of-class projects contribute to curriculum standards and essential learner goals? How?

_____

_____

_____

_____

• Do classroom activities enable me as the teacher to see knowledge in use and detect misconceptions? How?

_____

_____

_____

_____

- Are the learning materials in use in my class balanced in the way the standards (concepts, content, attitudes) are presented, or do they emphasize only one kind of learning and teaching?

_____

_____

- Do student performances reflect a balance in the ways that students can demonstrate curriculum standards? How?

_____

_____

- Do student assessments take a variety of approaches in measuring and reporting student achievement? How? Consider:
  - selected response items (tests and quizzes)
  - open-ended questions
  - performance-based assessments
  - products, rubrics, and task checklists

_____

_____

- Are students using appropriate technologies for locating, accessing, manipulating, and presenting information? How? Do these uses relate to the standards defined for our curriculum? How?

_____

_____

- How am I using our local community as a resource in achieving my curriculum standards? What programs, policies, people, and places can add value to the learning experiences of students in my school?

_____

_____

Step 4: Viewing Your Curriculum in the Larger Picture

You don't teach in a vacuum. Steps 1 through 3 have focused on your classroom. What about the larger picture?

Identify how your curriculum fits into the larger system. Answer the following questions to assess your school's (and your district's) response to standards.

- How familiar are our teachers with new standards or curriculum frameworks in their disciplines?

_____

_____

_____

_____

- Do we have equitable and prompt access to materials and current resources (not limited to textbooks) appropriate to achieving learner goals?

_____

_____

_____

_____

- Are we using time effectively and flexibly to achieve learning goals?
  - schedules built around instructional needs
  - teacher input
  - time built in for collaboration
  - maximizing the time spent learning

_____

_____

_____

_____

Step 5: Taking Action

List the action steps you need to take next in order to make your curriculum more "standards-based."

_____

_____

_____

_____

_____

_____

_____

_____

_____

_____

_____

_____

_____

_____

_____

_____

_____

_____

_____

_____

_____

_____

_____

_____

_____

_____

_____

_____

COMPACTING THE CURRICULUM

Curriculum compacting refers to the practice of letting students "qualify" for advancement within a regular course or to "test out" on certain academic requirements and move on to new material. That frees up the teacher to work more intensively with only those students who have not yet mastered essential skills or concepts. The three basic steps of curriculum compacting are:

- Identifying the major goals and objectives to be achieved.
- Determining which students have already mastered these goals.
- Re-ordering lessons, projects, or assignments to teach only those skills that students need to master and provide more time on new concepts.

Benefits of Curriculum Compacting

Students still "cover" the same essential objectives and contents of the planned course, but at differing rates and at different times, and in different groupings. Prior knowledge and rate of mastery of ideas create the differences. The content "covered" is the essentials and major ideas of a discipline rather than a range and depth of details. However, with a compacted curriculum, students have more opportunity to explore topics and interests in depth. They develop higher-level research and thinking skills.

As they function within a compacted curriculum, students gain additional skills in planning, managing, and evaluating independent studies. This is good practice for the adult world of work. Students are able to exercise more choices within their course of study and, as a result, along with developing skills, they develop an increased sense of responsibility for their own learning.

Defensible learning alternatives are absolutely critical to making the practice of curriculum compacting work. Deciding which learning alternatives to use and understanding each student's preferred learning styles, needs, and interests are a challenging part of your decision making in the curriculum compacting process.

A Possible Planning Sequence for Curriculum Compacting

Step 1: Identify the major, most essential learning objectives for a unit.

Step 2: Find out what students already know. Create a pretest for mastery of the major, most important objectives, using paper-and-pencil test or performance assessment.

Step 3: Record what each student knows and what skills/concepts each needs to work on.

Step 4: Provide targeted small group instruction or individualized instruction for students who have not yet mastered pretest objectives.

Step 5: Streamline practice time and reduce whole class instruction for students who have already learned the objectives.

Step 6: Offer enrichment activities or accelerated options for students who qualify based on the pretest such as:

- An accelerated curriculum based on advanced topics
- Individual or small group investigations
- Learning contracts
- Learning centers
- Seminar groups
- Mentor programs
- Self-directed units

Step 7: Keep records on the progress of each student and the instructional options each chooses. The data collected should provide evidence of:

- Student proficiency as verified by test scores or work performance
- Pretests used to determine mastery of major learning objectives
- Notation of the objectives that were eliminated
- Teacher recommendations for enrichment or acceleration

Freedom

Challenge

Conflict

Discovery

Change

Patterns

Relationships

The Future

Wellness

A unit theme may also be generative such as Immigration or the Rain Forest.

PLANNING INTEGRATED CURRICULUM

A block-of-time schedule provides an ideal framework for teaching interdisciplinary, thematic, or integrated curriculum, however it is titled in your district. Whether you are teaming or in a self-contained classroom, you will find that you now have the time to explore some of the topics and ideas of your subject area that have interested you for years. You will find that such an approach invigorates not only you but can motivate your students as they become active learners in the discovery process. The following planning tool will help you determine your theme and the strategies to develop it with your students.

An Integrated Curriculum Framework

Step 1: Determine the Organizing Center

What is our central theme? It may be a question, problem, or umbrella concept. In choosing an organizing center, think about:

- Ideas of significance
- Overarching concepts
- Unifying constructs
- Underlying metaphors
- Threads that weave through curriculum
- Questions that help students to interpret facts and events

State the theme as a question, problem or umbrella concept.

_____

Step 2: Cluster Guiding Questions

What related questions will serve to guide student inquiry, class activity, teaching, and learning? In a unit on the theme of family, the following essential questions were used to guide the unit structure:

- What is a family?
- How have roles and responsibilities of family members changed—and not changed—over generations?
- How can students view their family as a community and their community as a family?

Write at least three guiding questions for your unit.

1. _____

_____

2. _____

_____

3. _____

_____

Step 3: Identify Individual Tasks

Which learning tasks are best completed individually? What should be required of all students and what choices will students be able to make?

Here are some examples of individual tasks. Fill in the right-hand column with ideas that are specific to your unit.

_____ Draw a map   _____

_____ Compile a report   _____

_____ Make a collection   _____

_____ Write a critique   _____

_____ Conduct a guided tour   _____

Step 4: Select Small Group Tasks

What key products and performances would best be completed through team learning? Examples:

_____ Design a game   _____

_____ Build a model   _____

_____ Conduct an experiment   _____

_____ Present a skit   _____

_____ Examine an artifact   _____

Step 5: Choose Design and Technology Links

How can students discover that there is a design to the world by exploring the organizing center? How can students take that one step further and learn to locate, access, and manage information? Examples:

_____ Student inventions   _____

_____ Machines and structures   _____

_____ Models and prototypes   _____

_____ Databases   _____

_____ Information searches   _____

_____ Electronic discussion lists   _____

_____ Web sites   _____

Step 6: Sequence Whole Class Activity

What timeline of whole group meetings and events will let the unit unfold? Examples:

_____ Orientation meetings
to introduce the unit

_____

_____ Surveys of parents and
community members

_____

_____ Field trips

_____

_____ Guest speakers

_____

_____ Team exhibitions

_____

_____ Culminating activity or celebration

_____

Step 7. Plan Schoolwide Involvement

Is schoolwide involvement in some aspect of the unit possible? Is it desirable? Examples:

_____ Academic fair

_____

_____ Recycling project

_____

_____ Assembly

_____

Step 8. Make Community Connections

How can students learn in, from, and about their community? Examples:

_____ People they should know

_____

_____ Places they should visit

_____

_____ Policies they should examine

_____

_____ Programs they should know about

_____

_____ Practices they should question

_____

DEVELOPING A PACING GUIDE

How are you going to determine the key events, topics, concepts, skills, student projects, and performances that you will require your students to engage in for a semester? A pacing guide can show your best estimate for how long students will work on a particular unit of study in your class. This estimate will help you adjust your instructional practices, schedule your assessments, and anticipate materials, supplies, and other equipment and resource needs during the semester.

The Pacing Guide template on the next three pages suggests a rough way to depict how much time you will budget for a particular skill or concept. Feel free to add elements to it in ways that make sense for you. It might be helpful to share it with members of your department, your department chair, your curriculum or instructional coordinator, and/or your principal to get additional suggestions and comments.

Remember to revise your Pacing Guides after each semester to reflect what actually happened in the classroom.

A Pacing Guide

Week 1   Date _____

Themes/Concepts/Units _____

Texts/Chapters/Materials _____

Assessment _____

Week 2   Date _____

Themes/Concepts/Units _____

Texts/Chapters/Materials _____

Assessment _____

Week 3   Date _____

Themes/Concepts/Units _____

Texts/Chapters/Materials _____

Assessment _____

Week 4   Date _____

Themes/Concepts/Units _____

Texts/Chapters/Materials _____

Assessment _____

Week 5   Date _____

Themes/Concepts/Units _____

Texts/Chapters/Materials _____

Assessment _____

Week 6   Date _____

Themes/Concepts/Units _____

Texts/Chapters/Materials _____

Assessment _____

Week 7   Date _____

Themes/Concepts/Units _____

Texts/Chapters/Materials _____

Assessment _____

Week 8   Date _____

Themes/Concepts/Units _____

Texts/Chapters/Materials _____

Assessment _____

Week 9   Date _____

Themes/Concepts/Units _____

Texts/Chapters/Materials _____

Assessment _____

Week 10   Date _____

Themes/Concepts/Units _____

Texts/Chapters/Materials _____

Assessment _____

Week 11   Date _____

Themes/Concepts/Units _____

Texts/Chapters/Materials _____

Assessment _____

Week 12   Date _____

Themes/Concepts/Units _____

Texts/Chapters/Materials _____

Assessment _____

Week 13   Date _____

Themes/Concepts/Units _____

Texts/Chapters/Materials _____

Assessment _____

Week 14   Date _____

Themes/Concepts/Units _____

Texts/Chapters/Materials _____

Assessment _____

Week 15   Date _____

Themes/Concepts/Units _____

Texts/Chapters/Materials _____

Assessment _____

Week 16   Date _____

Themes/Concepts/Units _____

Texts/Chapters/Materials _____

Assessment _____

Week 17   Date _____

Themes/Concepts/Units _____

Texts/Chapters/Materials _____

Assessment _____

Week 18   Date _____

Themes/Concepts/Units _____

Texts/Chapters/Materials _____

Assessment _____

CHAPTER 3

"SHORT TAKES"

"SHORT TAKES"

Activities for providing brisk pacing, variety in classroom activities, and effective engagement of learners. These "take it, do it, show me what you know" activities form a major building block for effective use of learning time.

Group investigations provide students with opportunities to work in-depth and at-length on a topic or theme of their own choosing. There will be times, however, when you will want to draw on a different repertoire of shorter, interactive segments within a class period. Short activities like the ones suggested here make transitions between segments of instruction go more smoothly, as well as adding pacing and variety to the larger instructional "block." Active and engaging strategies such as these help students to remember more of what they have learned.

These tools can take the form of warm-up activities or "activators," providing learners with an opportunity to process the information that has just been presented, read, viewed, or encountered through direct, hands-on experience. "Energizers" can help "recharge" and add physical movement when students have been engaged in a task for longer periods of time. They can also serve as "summarizers," or closing activities, that give students an opportunity to reflect on new material and how it relates to what they have already learned.

In addition, these tools and strategies can be used to "set the stage" for learning new material, for providing guided or independent practice, class or team building, as well as feedback and assessment.

These activities can develop a life of their own. It is not the intent that the activities become your entire lesson! Be sure to stick with the suggested time frames, even if it means cutting discussions a little short. If your students have not had a great deal of experience with group and team work, consider beginning with the simpler strategies and moving on only as students demonstrate their increasing capacity for group work.

TURN TO YOUR NEIGHBOR
AND . . . (3-5 minutes)

"Turn to your neighbor and see if he or she agrees with the statement I have written on the board. If there is a disagreement, how can you use last night's assignment to prove the point?"

What are some statements from your discipline (could also be a formula, equation, diagram, or photograph) that you could use to stimulate dialogue between pairs of students in your class? Write them as you would on the board or on an acetate sheet for an overhead.

_____

_____

_____

_____

_____

_____

_____

_____

_____

_____

_____

_____

_____

_____

_____

_____

_____

_____

_____

_____

3-2-1 (3-5 minutes)

At the end of an explanation or demonstration, pass out index cards and have students write down:

- 3 important terms or ideas to remember
- 2 ideas or facts they would like to know more about
- 1 concept, process, or skill they think they have mastered

This activity can help make a transition to the next task, and lets you check quickly on progress.

Think of a lesson or segment of a lesson that you have taught recently or will be teaching soon.

- What 3 important terms or ideas would you like students to remember?
- What 2 ideas or facts do students often ask about?
- What 1 concept, process, or skill related to this lesson is easiest learned? Most difficult for students to grasp?

Predict how your students might complete a 3-2-1 card on your lesson.

_____

_____

_____

_____

_____

_____

_____

_____

_____

_____

_____

_____

_____

_____

TICKET TO LEAVE
(3-5 minutes)

This "short take" is especially good when an activity concludes just before the end of a period. Pass out a printed "ticket" about the size of a half sheet of notebook paper. Ask each student to jot down two additional questions about the topic that was just explained or investigated in some way. This activity reinforces the assumption that you are never finished learning and should continue to ask questions and seek information. Collect the tickets and use them to review the topic.

Put yourself in the role of the student. Complete a ticket to leave on a lesson that you have recently taught or will be teaching soon.

TICKET

_____

_____

_____

_____

_____

_____

_____

_____

_____

_____

_____

_____

_____

_____

_____

_____

A NOTE TO A FRIEND
(5-10 minutes)

At the end of an explanation or demonstration, have students take a sheet of paper and write a note to a friend explaining the process, rule, or concept they have just learned about. Have students share these restatements.

Try writing a note to a friend explaining why block lessons must include student-to-student interaction.

_____

_____

_____

_____

_____

_____

_____

_____

_____

_____

_____

_____

_____

_____

_____

_____

_____

_____

SORT THE ITEMS
(5-10 minutes)

Ask students to place ideas, concepts, or statements in categories that you provide. For example, you might ask "Which statements were based on fact?" and "Which statements were based on inference?" This is a good activity to use to teach skills and content together.

Think about the key skills required in your course. What skills will help students sort the information and learn concepts, for example, recognizing cause and effect, comparing and contrasting, and/or predicting and estimating? List those key skills.

_____

_____

_____

_____

_____

_____

_____

_____

_____

_____

_____

_____

_____

_____

_____

_____

_____

_____

JUMBLED SUMMARY
(5-10 minutes)

Write key words or phrases from an explanation or introduction in random order on an acetate sheet or on a page to be photocopied. Following the presentation, ask pairs to "unscramble" the terms and reorder them in logical sequence as a knowledge check.

Write down in a logical, linear sequence key words or phrases related to some concept you have taught recently or will be teaching. Now scramble them to create a list your students can reorder in proper sequence.

PREDICTION PAIRS
(5-10 minutes)

Divide the class into pairs and have students work in pairs as they listen to a short story you are reading aloud. Read a short passage, then pause to ask the prediction pairs to state "What will happen next?" and "What are your reasons for this prediction, based on the story so far?"

List some short stories, brief passages, or narrative that you can read aloud in segments, pausing to ask students for their predictions.

_____

_____

_____

_____

_____

_____

_____

_____

_____

_____

_____

_____

_____

_____

_____

_____

_____

_____

_____

_____

_____

ALPHABET SUMMARY
(5-10 minutes)

At the end of an explanation or demonstration, give each student a different letter of the alphabet and ask students to think of one word or idea beginning with that letter that is connected to the topic just concluded. Use the responses for a whole class discussion review.

Using a topic, concept, or theme that your class has studied, generate a list of key words and put them in alphabetical order. Try the "short take" for a lesson you are about to teach.

_____

_____

_____

_____

_____

_____

_____

_____

_____

_____

_____

_____

_____

_____

_____

_____

_____

_____

THINK-PAIR-SHARE
(5-10 minutes)

After an explanation or demonstration, distribute index cards to students, and ask them to think about what they have just heard. Have them write down three statements about it on the index card and exchange their responses with a partner. Have the whole class debrief on the topic. Ask for frequently mentioned ideas or terms.

Write your ideas for a Think-Pair-Share on a topic you have taught or are about to teach.

_____

_____

_____

_____

_____

_____

_____

_____

_____

_____

_____

_____

_____

_____

_____

_____

_____

_____

DRAW A PICTURE
(5-10 minutes)

At the end of a segment of teacher-directed instruction, ask participants to work in pairs to create a graphic summary of how they would organize information, reach a conclusion, or interact differently based on the demonstration you just provided.

What are some graphic organizers your students use? Which ones would you like to teach them?

_____

_____

_____

_____

_____

_____

_____

_____

_____

_____

_____

_____

_____

_____

_____

_____

_____

_____

_____

THREE-PERSON JIGSAW
(15 minutes)

Each student in a trio reads a separate page or a portion of a longer selection. Then he or she teaches the main points to the two other members of their study group. Each then quizzes the other members to make sure everyone know all parts thoroughly.

Can you identify three different related articles or chapter segments that you could assign in a three-person jigsaw?

_____

_____

_____

_____

_____

_____

_____

_____

_____

_____

_____

_____

_____

_____

_____

_____

_____

_____

_____

_____

_____

_____

_____

K-W-L TRIO
(15 minutes)

Before a film, lecture, or reading, have students work in threes to write down what they already *know* about the subject and what they *want* to *learn* about the subject. Then show the film, deliver the lecture, or engage the group in the reading. Have each trio:

- circle the "known" information that was covered
- put asterisks next to the questions that were answered on their list
- add other things they learned as a result of the film, lecture, or reading.

From your students' point of view, develop a K-W-L chart on a topic you will be introducing in your classroom.

_____

_____

_____

_____

_____

_____

_____

_____

_____

_____

_____

_____

_____

_____

_____

_____

DRILL PARTNERS
(15 minutes)

Form pairs and have students drill each other on facts they need to recall until they are certain both partners know and can remember them all. This works effectively with vocabulary terms; sight recognition of birds, leaves, mathematical symbols, and shapes; and grammar.

List the topics or skills you can have students help each other learn through repetition and recitation.

_____

_____

_____

_____

_____

_____

_____

_____

_____

_____

_____

_____

_____

_____

_____

_____

_____

WRITING RESPONSE PAIRS
(20 minutes)

In this "short take" students read and respond to each other's written work:

- by marking passages that they think are effective with a star
- by underlining what they don't understand or think is weak
- by circling errors in grammar, usage, punctuation, spelling, or format.

Then the reader discusses his/her observations with the writer.

What are some writing assignments that you typically give to students that can be reviewed in writing response pairs?

_____

_____

_____

_____

_____

_____

_____

_____

_____

_____

_____

_____

_____

_____

_____

_____

_____

_____

INSIDE-OUTSIDE CIRCLES
(10-20 minutes)

Organize students into groups of six, with three students standing in a circle and facing out, and three students forming a circle around them, facing inward. Each student faces another student. Direct each pair to exchange information related to yesterday's lesson, the unit so far, etc. You may also provide questions to stimulate dialogue. Then ask the students in the center circle to rotate, facing a new partner, and choose a different topic for exchange.

Choose a general topic from your discipline or specific content from a unit, and write down three questions that you would have opposite pairs discuss in each of three turns of the circle.

_____

_____

_____

_____

_____

_____

_____

_____

_____

_____

_____

_____

_____

_____

_____

_____

_____

FOUR CORNERS
(15-20 minutes)

This is an especially effective activity in social studies, language arts, or science courses, where students encounter controversial issues. State a situation or dilemma, then ask students to go to one of four corners of the room, marked Strongly Agree, Agree, Strongly Disagree, Disagree. There students exchange their opinions or reasoning, and summarize their reasoning for presentation to the other three corners.

List three situations or dilemmas from your subject area for which "Four Corners" would be a useful activity to help students sharpen their reasoning and practice considering others' opinions.

_____

_____

_____

_____

_____

_____

_____

_____

_____

_____

_____

_____

_____

_____

NUMBERED HEADS TOGETHER
(10 minutes)

Group students by teams. Each team member counts off, so that each member has a number. Ask a question or present a problem, and allow the teams time to agree jointly on the correct answer.

Then select a team and call a number at random. The student with that number must answer the question and briefly explain why that answer is correct.

If the group has not been able to arrive at a joint answer, the team must "pass" until it is called upon again. "Numbered Heads" can be especially useful when reviewing large "chunks" of material or in helping students prepare for a test.

Generate a list of five problems or questions for this activity based on your current unit.

_____

_____

_____

_____

_____

_____

_____

_____

_____

_____

_____

_____

_____

_____

_____

_____

PAIRS CHECK
(10-20 minutes)

Divide the class into pairs. One student in the pair works on a task while the other serves as coach. Then they exchange roles for the second task. At this point, they ask another pair to check their work. If the second pair agrees with their response, the first pair continues. If not, the pair tries to correct their work.

List three homework assignments you routinely assign where the technique "Pairs Check" would be useful.

_____

_____

_____

_____

_____

_____

_____

_____

_____

_____

_____

_____

_____

_____

_____

_____

_____

_____

_____

_____

_____

ROUNDTABLE
(10-20 minutes)

Ask a question with many possible answers ("Name all of the items in your home that were not invented 25 years ago."). Using one sheet of paper, students make a list, each person adding one item and then passing the paper to the person on his/her left. The product is the result of many minds (and hands) at work, hence "Roundtable." You can use this technique with teams of several students each.

Write the questions and directions for a "Roundtable" activity related to a topic in your current lesson or unit.

_____

_____

_____

_____

_____

_____

_____

_____

_____

_____

_____

_____

_____

_____

_____

_____

_____

_____

_____

SEND-A-PROBLEM
(10-20 minutes)

Each student on a team makes up a question or review problem and writes it on a flashcard. The author of each problem/question asks the question of his/her team members. If consensus is not reached on the answer, the group works on the problem or rewords it until everyone can explain/agree. After all the flashcards have been reviewed, the team passes its stack of review questions to another team for review.

With which unit or topic in your curriculum would this technique work best? List several possible units or topics.

_____

_____

_____

_____

_____

_____

_____

_____

_____

_____

_____

_____

_____

_____

_____

_____

_____

GROUP TEST TAKING
FOR PRACTICE (20 minutes)

The day before a test, give student groups copies of earlier versions of your test or questions similar to those that will actually be on the test. Tell them that "Tomorrow as individuals you will get a test like this. There will be no team to help you, but you can help one another today. Coach your teammates so everyone will do well tomorrow."

For which chapters, units, or topics do you have several versions of tests? List your resources here.

_____

_____

_____

_____

_____

_____

_____

_____

_____

_____

_____

_____

_____

_____

_____

_____

_____

TIMED-PAIR-SHARE
(5-10 minutes)

Have students pair off according to some specific, predetermined criterion: "Students who did not see the televised debate last night pair off with someone who did," "Students who agree that Montressa was justified pair off with those who sympathize with Fortunato," "Students who play a musical instrument or have taken music lessons pair off with students who have not." Then give explicit directions to the pairs for some task. For example:

- "Partner #1 has two minutes to explain why he/she believes candidate A or candidate B carried the debate. Partner #2 has two minutes to ask questions about other aspects of the debate before we get to the main part of today's lesson."

- "Partner #1 has two minutes to explain why he/she thinks Montressa was justified. Partner #2 has two minutes to explain why Fortunato was a victim."

The Timed-Pair-Share activity adds structure and time limits to ensure that each member of the pair has equal opportunity to participate.

Generate some timed-pair-share assignments that you could use with your current unit or lesson. Keep your directions brief.

_____

_____

_____

_____

_____

_____

_____

_____

_____

_____

ROUND-THE-CLOCK LEARNING BUDDIES
(5-10 minutes per interaction)

Distribute to each student a sheet of paper with the face of a clock printed on it. Next to each hour place a horizontal line. Direct students to identify three different learning buddies with whom to confer during the lesson: one at 9 o'clock, one at 12 o'clock, and one at 3 o'clock. The student pairs write each other's names in the spaces provided. As the lesson unfolds, the teacher directs the class to "meet with your 9 o'clock learning buddy to review the major ideas we have just covered," "meet with your 12 o'clock buddy to compare your reasons for disagreeing with the author's point of view," and "meet with your 3 o'clock learning buddy to cite specific evidence from your laboratory experience to support the claim that not all cells contain a nucleus."

The use of "Round-the-Clock Learning Buddies" in the examples provided show how brief interactions can help students process information they have just acquired, make critical judgments about what they are learning, and develop habits of precision and accuracy in using evidence from first-hand observation.

Write directions for "one at 9 o'clock, one at 12 o'clock, and one at 3 o'clock" that can be used for reviewing a chapter or unit.

_____

_____

_____

_____

_____

_____

_____

_____

_____

_____

IDEA SPINNER
(5-10 minutes)

Construct a "spinner" made from cardboard (a stiff piece of paper and pizza wheel work well) marked into four quadrants: summarize, explain, predict, evaluate. Following the presentation of new material, call on different students and use the spinner to frame questions based on the information presented (could be a demonstration, videotape, skit, or lecture). For example:

- Summarize: "What was the main idea in . . ."
- Explain: "Give a step-by-step description of . . ."
- Predict: "What do you think would have happened if . . ."
- Evaluate: "Which of the following two choices do you think is . . ."

"Idea Spinner" will help you raise a variety of questions and look at a topic through different "lenses."

Which topics or units you teach would be best investigated using "Idea Spinner"? Complete the prompts above using one of these topics or units.

_____

_____

_____

_____

_____

_____

_____

_____

_____

_____

_____

_____

HOW ARE WE DOING?
(5-10 minutes)

Distribute to each student a sheet with the following writing prompts:

- Three things that have helped me learn today are . . .
- One thing the teacher could do to help me learn more is . . .
- One thing I could do to help myself learn more about this topic is . . .

This "short take" provides feedback to help you better determine what help students might need in mastering essential concepts and skills.

What do you think your students might write if you used this technique?

_____

_____

_____

_____

_____

_____

_____

_____

_____

_____

_____

_____

_____

_____

SUMMING UP (5 minutes)

Group activities do not have to take a long time. You can organize students into pairs or threes and ask them to do any one of the following in five minutes, at the most!

- Describe what they have just heard about a topic.

- Explain important points or distinctions to each other.

- Compare responses to a hypothetical situation you provide.

- List the attributes of a condition or skill, or make up rules for governing a situation.

- Predict what will happen if . . .

- Estimate the consequences of . . .

- Identify patterns in . . .

Think about your subject area. How could you use each prompt above to have your students "sum up" lessons?

_____

_____

_____

_____

_____

_____

_____

_____

_____

_____

_____

_____

_____

"BLOCKING" LESSONS: A CLASSROM CHOREOGRAPHY

"How do I spend 90 minutes with students in a way that maximizes the opportunity to learn, keeps students on-task, and doesn't drive me nuts in the process?"

These are some questions that teachers typically ask when they face the transition from shorter class periods (40-50 minutes) to longer periods (80-120 minutes) of learning time. This chapter provides some practical tools, tips, and techniques for getting the most out of block-of-time learning. Chapter 5 describes ways to use small group or cooperative learning strategies, a vital instructional element for problem- and project-based learning. There are two things to keep in mind regardless of the strategies that you use: Save your voice for the important things and post a daily class agenda.

See Appendix A, "Checklist of Action Steps for Teaching in a Block-Scheduled Classroom," to help you put into the practice the tips and tools in this chapter.

SAVE YOUR VOICE

In Chapter 1, we talked about the need to prepare yourself for the physical strain of teaching in the block. One of your most important physical resources is your voice. Don't waste it on classroom routines. To reiterate what we said in Chapter 1, at the beginning of the course, establish class routines and procedures and make sure you communicate them clearly to your students as your expectations for appropriate behavior. Some suggested routines to help your voice are:

- Use your voice for clear explanations and giving good examples of the ideas that you are trying to convey.
- Write instructions for individual or group work on the board or on an acetate for overhead projection.
- Use an agreed-upon signal to get students' attention.

POST A DAILY AGENDA

Another suggestion in Chapter 1 was to post a daily agenda to provide your students with an immediate overview of what will happen in the class that day and what they are expected to do. This is especially important when students are expected to take charge of their own learning through project work. You can post the agenda on newsprint, the board, or an overhead. Your daily class agenda may include:

30 minutes	Introduction of new topic, concept, and/or skill as demonstration to the whole class with student interaction
30 minutes	Review by cooperative groups of the concept, topic, or skill presented
30 minutes	Whole group discussion/debrief on previous topic and introduction of new, related concept

A sample agenda might look like:

9:00-9:30	Teacher demonstration of new topic to whole class
9:30-10:00	Cooperative group review of topic
10:00-10:30	Whole class discussion/debrief and new lesson

USING TIME FOR
THE MAXIMUM EFFECT

If all of your classes are the same length, you may start out with a set of short whole group "warm ups" and close with a set of whole group "cool downs." Math classes often start out with a problem of the day for which individuals or teams may earn "points."

If your block-schedule classes are of different lengths or on different days, you may do your planning around the length of time available, such that the shorter sessions are used for review, exhibitions or performance, or formal testing. The routines should reflect the rhythm and language of the discipline. For example, laboratory investigations generally follow some introductory experiences or explorations, providing students with practical opportunities to observe scientific principles in action.

How can I organize my teaching strategies according to the way my schedule is set up?

_____

_____

_____

_____

_____

_____

_____

_____

_____

_____

_____

_____

_____

_____

LEARNING STATIONS

Learning stations are a good way to organize time. They provide the needed change in routine while moving students around in an orderly fashion. They can also maximize the use of scarce equipment or other resources. If you have only one computer in your room, make it one of the learning stations. Both cooperative learning groups (see Chapter 5) and learning stations provide hands-on learning experiences, require that students practice essential knowledge and skills, free you up to observe and assess learning, and are more likely to meet the needs of individual students.

To use learning stations, divide the class into learning teams and rotate the teams through a series of learning stations that require the teams to perform a key task related to the topic under study at each learning station. Here is a sample timeline:

15 minutes	Introduction of the lesson and instructions for using the learning stations
15 minutes	Station 1
15 minutes	Station 2
15 minutes	Station 3
15 minutes	Station 4
15 minutes	Review and refinement of the learning by each group; possible use of a "short take"

This assumes that the next class period will deal with a review to ensure that students have understood the material. A "short take" such as "Ticket to Leave" could be a useful device for providing continuity between this session and the next meeting of the class.

What are some ways I could organize learning stations in my classroom?

_____

_____

_____

_____

_____

_____

WORKSHOPS

The workshop format provides a variety of activities and changes of pace while providing time for in-depth content/concept and writing skills work. Even if you are not a language arts or reading teacher, try it in your subject area. A sample set of activities might look like this:

15 minutes   Sustained silent reading (Everybody reads.)

15 minutes   Reader response forms (Everybody writes in response to an analysis of the reading selection.)

30 minutes   Choices (Everybody must do one of the following.):
- journal reflections
- peer review or a required essay/product
- research (including a pass to the library/media center to do multimedia searches)
- conference with the teacher (oral discussion of work in progress)
- publishing center (final print-out of work in progress)
- presentation rehearsal (practice/feedback with peer or small group)

30 minutes   Whole group instruction (This may include your reading to the class, the class reading to you, discussion of story/themes, critical review of the reading, etc.)

What choices would you provide for your students?

_____

_____

_____

_____

_____

_____

_____

_____

ASSESSMENT

It can't be stated enough: Assessment should be part of the instructional process. Build into your instructional time opportunities for students to:

- Add materials to their portfolios.
- Have a personal conference with you.
- Review a videotape of their performance to assess how well they execute a procedure. Use an agreed upon rubric for the self-assessment.
- "Qualify" for points or credit by completing a performance (may be a demonstration to a group of elementary students, a presentation to another class, or a community service project).
- Work on independent or group projects resulting in some tangible product such as a poster, diorama, working model, construction, report, multimedia presentation, video, database, etc.

What kinds of assessment activities can I do more of in my classroom?

_____

_____

_____

_____

_____

_____

_____

_____

_____

_____

_____

_____

_____

_____

_____

PROBLEM-CENTERED INSTRUCTION

Many adult occupations deal with resolving problems—in law, medicine, agriculture, industry, business, finance, and government. By putting students in the roles of scientists, reporters, writers, artists, historians, mathematicians, and judges, you help your students integrate the acquisition of basic skills with career exploration and the development of a life-long learning interest. To use real-world problems, let students address a concept, problem, or issue that they are likely to encounter in life beyond the classroom. Such a problem situation challenges your students to think more deeply, apply learning to real-life situations, examine the information they discover, and use their knowledge to construct ethical solutions to problems.

Example: (from an individual mathematics task)

We are making a bookcase to hold our new stereo. We need to have three shelves. The top shelf must contain three compartments; the second shelf, two compartments; the bottom shelf, one compartment. We also have 6 boards that are 60 inches long, 2 1/2 inches wide, and 1 inch thick. You may use only the materials provided. Draw a diagram of what the bookcase will look like when finished. Use fractions to show how you will cut the boards to make the compartments.

What are some possible real-life problems related to my subject area that students could investigate?

PROJECT-CENTERED INSTRUCTION

Projects help students learn to manage time in group work, solve problems together, integrate content, and develop life-long work habits. Usually, a project will result in some tangible product: a written report, a display, a collection, a poster, a construction or model, or a performance or presentation. Often a project is designed in such a way that the students communicate their knowledge through a product or performance for an audience beyond the teacher, classroom, and school building. The product becomes the major assessment instrument from project-related work.

Example: (from a social studies class)

The Immigration Debate

A major debate is on-going about whether the United States can continue to welcome immigrants at the current rate of 800,000 a year. Some believe that immigration is a major drain on the economy, while others believe that immigrants add to the gross domestic product. The debate has economic, political, sociological, and moral aspects.

- Task: As background, do research on the history of immigration to the United States beginning with the 1840s, the changes in the laws since the 1870s and why they have occurred, and identify the current points of view on the subject of immigration. Use this information to construct an argument either for or against continuing the U.S.'s current immigration policy.

- Presentation: Your product may take any form that will present your case persuasively such as an oral presentation before a Congressional committee, a booklet or special report prepared by a public policy group, a slide show before a public policy group, a special report, etc. You have to identify your point of view, create a group to convey that point of view, and determine how best to get your message to others.

- Resources: Use the *Statistical Abstract,* nonfiction books including first-person accounts and histories, news magazines, newspapers; use at least six sources.

What topics/concepts/issues in my discipline would lend themselves to projects? List the topics/concepts/issues and then the kind of projects that would work for each one.

_____

_____

_____

AUTHENTIC ASSIGNMENTS

Authentic assignments serve to motivate as well as deepen students' understanding by exploring concepts and skills with thoroughness. Through authentic assignments, students perform the same activities that successful adults, such as scientists, musicians, business managers, novelists, nurses, and designers do. Assignments should be set up in such a way that students are able to demonstrate their knowledge in a culminating performance or product. Throughout the process, the teacher's role is to encourage students to self-assess, self-evaluate, and self-regulate their own work—as adults do in the workplace.

> Example: (from an environmental science class)
>
> Select one of the neighborhoods marked on the city map. Identify its current features by doing an inventory of its buildings, businesses, housing, and public facilities. Identify current transportation patterns and traffic flow. Describe any environmental problems the neighborhood is experiencing such as traffic flow, drainage back up, incinerator discharge, abandoned cars. As a group, choose one problem and consider various plans for changing and improving the situation.

What are some workplace tasks my students can perform that mirror on-the-job situations?

_____

_____

_____

_____

_____

_____

_____

_____

_____

_____

VARYING
QUESTIONING TECHNIQUES

When you ask your students open-ended questions, they have to manipulate information and ideas by using analysis, synthesis, and evaluation as well as recall, comprehension, and application (Bloom's Taxonomy is still alive and well.). Such questions stimulate all forms of thinking including higher order thought processes. Different types of questions help students learn how to organize their thinking about content. Such variety also encourages students to think about their own thinking. By varying your questioning strategies, you as the teacher are also able to respond to students' learning preferences.

> Example: (from the previous environmental science project)
>
> After deciding on a plan, draw and label it on the overlay provided with your map. (technique 1) Indicate in a written narrative one possible plan you rejected, and explain why you rejected it. (technique 2) How will your plan promote and achieve the neighborhood improvement your group chose?(technique 3)

Some things to think about:
- "Do or does" questions usually result in one-word answers.
- "How and why" questions usually result in explanations.

What are some kinds of questions I would like to use more of in my subject area?

_____

_____

_____

_____

_____

_____

_____

_____

_____

_____

INTEGRATING TECHNOLOGY

The power of technology can energize and motivate students—and teachers. By providing classroom opportunities for your students to use and make a variety of tools to gather, analyze, and manipulate data, you can help your students make connections between what they are learning in school and workplace skills required in the world beyond school. If the only software you have is a spreadsheet or database program, your students can still create their own information tools.

One way to use technology in the classroom is to have students use software, CD-ROMs, laser disks, and multimedia to enhance project-based learning and authentic assessment. Another is to require students to show the results of their work in a product or presentation using technology.

Example of technology as an instructional support (from a social studies class using *The Decisions, Decisions* Series available for MAC, APPLE II, or MS-DOS, from Tom Synder Productions, Inc., Cambridge, MA):

Students become presidents of countries faced with international relations dilemmas or massive immigration problems, or town mayors faced with environmental crises. "On-line advisors" point students to opinions, facts, precedents, and advice drawn from history and current events. Students are exposed to all sides of the issues and learn the complexities involved in decision making. Students learn to set priorities, think critically about the data they read and work with, make connections, and anticipate consequences in order to make their decisions.

- Students uncover a real-world dilemma through an on-line presentation and critical reading of the scenario in their reference books.
- As a whole group, students prioritize their goals.
- On-line advisors point students to relevant historical references and offer multiple perspectives on the decisions the students face.
- Opposing viewpoints and examples from the past spark classroom discussions as students come to a consensus on what action to take.
- The computer presents the actual consequences and advisors reappear to offer additional help.

What are some promising applications of technology in my discipline?

_____

_____

STUDENT DIALOGUE

Teachers who emphasize logic, reasoning, and effective communication require students to engage in substantive conversation with the teacher and/or peers in a way that builds improved and shared understanding of ideas and topics. Such conversations are characterized by discussing different points of view openly, seeking solutions mutually, creating positive and productive relationships.

Socratic Seminars are a specialized format for generating critical thinking and essential questioning. While the rest of the class works on individual projects or rehearsals, the teacher might work with 10 to 15 students who have completed a major reading (a novel, case, or essay) in a seminar format. The teacher prepares for the seminar by constructing questions based on the reading assignment for which:

- there could be many possible responses.
- the leader does not have all the answers.
- all participants can respond (round robin, voting).

Example: (from an English class)
- What did the author mean by "_____?"
- How would you rate "_____?"
- Can you find a passage in the text that supports that position?
- How is "_____" different from "_____?"
- How does this relate to today?
- What two or three themes have come up repeatedly in our discussion?

If you are not a language arts teacher, how could you foster dialogue among and between your students and you about your subject area material? Some questions I can ask to extend my students' thinking are:

_____

_____

_____

_____

_____

_____

CONTRACTS

Most of what we've talked about so far relates to group work, although projects and problems can also be assigned as individual work. All work in a block-of-time schedule does not have to be geared toward group work. Individual and individualized work are still important. Using a contract system in which a student promises to do a set amount of work in a set amount of time can be useful, especially in a heterogeneously grouped class.

Among the advantages of contracts is that time is not such an important variable in student learning. Students work at their own pace, and in so doing they learn to manage their own time. They also learn to make choices about their activities.

Good contracts:

- are designed to meet specific curriculum objectives;
- offer instructional alternatives to meet learning styles, interests, and ability levels;
- present choices for students;
- enable teachers to customize, individualize learning.

  Example: (from language arts/English):

  During this week, you must accumulate twenty-five (25) points by Friday. You may choose any of the activities you wish in order to accumulate your points.

  - I will write a letter to one of the characters from my book, telling him/her how I feel about how he/she is handling the situation in the book. This letter must be at least one page in length. (10 points)
  - I will design an advertisement for the book I am reading, trying to "sell" it to other students to read. (15 points)
  - I will write a letter to the author of the book I am reading, telling him/her what I thought of the book and why. The letter must be at least two pages in length and discuss plot and character. (25 points)
  - and so on.

What kinds of tasks would be appropriate for contracts in my subject area?

_____

_____

_____

LEARNING LOGS

Learning logs or journals provide another avenue for individual work regardless of the subject area. They are as valuable for self-reflection, self-evaluation, and getting students to think about their own thinking in math classes as they are in English/language arts. Learning logs can be used for:

- self-assessment to evaluate individual progress in a class.
- personal reactions to lectures, readings, viewings, recordings, working of problems, and similar kinds of activities.
- reflection on one's contributions to a group project, discussion, etc.
- recording questions, observations, insights in preparation for a student-teacher conference.
- recording ideas for reports, research projects, essays, short stories, poems, etc., to be developed later.
- commenting on ideas learned or making connections among subject matter.
- describing specific incidents and impressions arising from special events, guest speakers, and field trips.

How could I structure my classes to make use of learning logs?

_____

_____

_____

_____

_____

_____

_____

_____

_____

_____

_____

_____

SMALL GROUP LEARNING STRATEGIES

Small group or cooperative group work is an essential element of learning-based instruction and can provide the variety and motivation that will help your block-scheduled classes succeed. Dividing classes into smaller groups that work on the same or different tasks provides several benefits to students. First, they learn the skills of group work by using roles, following rules, keeping records, and focusing on results. Second, students can review what you have just taught, or can build on prior knowledge by pursuing something new. Third, like learning stations, cooperative groups provide hands-on learning experiences that require practice of essential skills and knowledge. Group work is also more likely to meet individual student needs.

See Appendix B for "Checklist for Monitoring and Assessing Small Group Learning."

PURPOSEFUL GROUP WORK

There are a variety of small group learning structures that contribute to increased student learning and productive use of classroom time. Here are some specific examples of small groups at work:

- *Study groups* review previously taught material in preparation for a teacher-made test or quiz.
- *Drill teams/drill partners* serve as coaches and trainers to each other to learn new material.
- *Problem-solving teams* propose, build, and test a solution to a problem by making drawings, models, and prototypes.
- *Laboratory teams* carry out experiments and inquiries by sharing observations, procedures, conclusions, and materials.
- *Research teams* conduct investigations by sharing ideas, information, and responsibilities.

- *Expert panels* are groups of students who have become expert in some aspect of a class study or unit.
- *Enactment groups* are teams of students who prepare, rehearse, and present a reenactment of a significant literary, historical, or scientific event to the rest of the class or an audience beyond the class.
- *Shop/lab/studio helpers* are student leader teams, pairs, or trios of students who serve as work group supervisors in a course for younger students.
- *Interdisciplinary investigation team,* sometimes called "area studies" teams, are grouped by interest or the skills required to complete a study of a community resource.
- *Debate teams* research a controversial issue and marshal arguments for and against a particular position.
- In a *jigsaw team,* each student has something that he or she reads and "teaches" to the others in the group.
- In *student teams achievement divisions,* the teacher presents (teaches) new information, which the students review (study) in teams, followed by a test and recognition (certificate) of team performance.
- In *team/games/tournament structures,* the teacher presents (teaches) new information, which students review (study) in teams, followed by a game (tournament) in which students are matched by ability and get points for their study team. This is followed by recognition (certificate) of team performance.

PREPARING STUDENTS FOR WORKING IN GROUPS

To have successful small group learning experiences in your class:
- Make group work purposeful.
- Prepare students for success.
- Keep flexible and be vigilant.

Because many students are not used to working in groups, it is important that you teach, model, and assess the skills of teamwork as if they were the content of the class. Especially important are social skills: listening, taking turns, encouraging, supporting one another, staying on task, cleaning up the work area, etc. Beginning with simpler tasks for teams and building to more complex assignments is an effective way of building capacity.

In designing an activity, pick the right-sized task for your class. It must be challenging enough to keep students interested, but easy enough for students to achieve success (with effort) in the time allotted. Not every group will finish at the same time, however. As suggested in Chapter 1, have a classroom poster or handout with a list of "What to Do If You Finish Early" items on it for those groups that finish ahead of the allotted time.

In designing group work, it is important to change the composition of groups frequently so that students of different backgrounds, academic achievement levels, and social skills learn to work together. This mixing and matching will build familiarity, insights, and trust among class members. Organizing the work so that each team member contributes to the achievement of the team goals also builds a sense of individual—and group—responsibility. It makes every member of the group an important member.

If a project is to last over a period of time, it is easy for inexperienced groups to let assignments slide. It's useful, therefore, to hold groups accountable for completing specific tasks or project steps during work sessions. Include a very specific assignment or menu of options for teams to work on. "Every meeting results in a product," whether it is a list to create, a diagram to draw, an outline to display, a form to fill out, etc. This strategy also promotes group responsibility.

While you as the teacher will be using observations, tests, checklists, and individual assignments to measure each student's achievement, it's important that team members also assess their own work. Two important outcomes of alternative approaches in student assessment are better understanding of self and increased responsibility for one's own learning. You will need to provide opportunities for both individuals and groups to use self-assessment tools, to reflect on progress over time, and to set new goals for performance. Teams need to assess how well they work together and what improvements they might make, and individual members need to assess how their actions contribute to the overall team. Reflection should be seen as part of every activity.

YOUR ROLE

Your role as organizer and facilitator of the groups is very important. Much of what you will need to do is the same as what happens in planning for individual or whole group work. For example, you will still need to analyze the information to be learned to determine what strategies are the most effective. If you determine that small group work is the best way, then you will need to determine what tasks the groups will need to do. What are the learning objectives? What content, skills, or attitudes should students be able to demonstrate? How much and what kind of practice will students need in order to demonstrate their new skills and knowledge?

Use flexible grouping strategies so that students do not always work in the same groups. Some strategies for forming groups are:
- Teacher-determined groups
- Student-determined groups
- Teacher- and student-determined groups
- Chance-determined groups
- Skill/interest-determined groups

IDEAS FOR DEVELOPING SMALL GROUP WORK

- **Introduce the unit or project to the whole class at once.**
  In this way everyone knows what the different groups will be working on and can get "the big picture" view of how various components of the unit or the project fit together.

- **Require students to construct something.**
  The construction of a model, a prototype, sketch or drawing, etc., should give you insights into how students perceive concepts, time, history, etc.

- **Offer both required tasks and student choices.**
  Offering students more latitude in choosing the topic to investigate and the format for reporting/demonstrating their learning can provide motivation.

- **Have students learn from first-hand experience.**
  Part of the time have students survey parents, students, faculty, or community members in order to generate new data for their research. Again, this strategy can be motivating and it also provides a real-world connection to what they are learning.

- **Expect students to conduct library research** in which they
  - use at least three sources for their research (e.g., books, personal interviews, articles, newspaper reports, etc.).
  - construct an argument for or against the issue, citing their sources.
  - present the argument to an audience beyond the classroom.
  - present the argument using visual aids, a pamphlet prepared for the public, oral presentation, a slide show, etc. Encourage creative ideas.

- **Have students keep a journal or daily learning log in which they write responses to specific prompts that you provide.**

- **Assign tasks that require students to read, write, reflect, listen, speak, construct, or perform during part of their group work.**

- **Plan a culminating activity.**
  A trip to a museum, visit to a tidepool or mountain top, or field investigation such as testing water quality at a local pool or pond explores community/regional resources and provides a real-world link.

- **Require students to present, report, or demonstrate their learning.**
  At the end of the unit provide a range of options for students to choose from, but ensure that students try each option at least once during the school year. Options could include a media demonstration; videotape; written report; oral report; a performance such as a song, dance or skit; hands-on demonstration; model or prototype; project; display; design or drawing.

Evaluating progress and encouraging self-assessment are very important aspects of the teacher's role with small groups. Some of the questions to ask yourself are: What standards must small groups achieve? What criteria will I use to determine that the task has been successfully completed? What rubric or rating scale will let me assess individual or group proficiency in executing the desired skill or demonstrating the required knowledge? As stated in the previous section, you will also need to provide opportunities for both individual and group self-assessments.

Chapter 1 advised that block-of-time scheduling might require a change in classroom arrangements. This is certainly true if you are using small group work. Small group work often requires a different arrangement of chairs, desks, and tables. As one of your new classroom routines, you may need to devise a procedure for moving students and their furniture into groups as they come in to class. You may also need systems for storing and retrieving papers, materials, and supplies. The noise level in your classroom may also increase as students teach one another, quiz each other, review materials and ideas together, and practice presentations. You may need to alert your fellow teachers and your administration.

A final word on teacher as coach. Small group work requires critical and creative thinking that many students may not have. You can provide these tools as team advisor or coach or can integrate them in a work session warm up at the beginning of a class. The teacher's role during small group work is to serve as monitor, supervisor, and coach. Sometimes the coach must blow the whistle and redirect the group, so it can complete the assignment. Times to intervene are when:

- the group is off task.
- the group is having difficulty beginning or completing the task.
- the group experiences interpersonal conflict.
- the group cannot organize to get the work done.

AN EXAMPLE

Page 80 presents an example of how a small group activity, Jigsaw, could be used in a block-of-time period.

JIGSAW: EXAMPLE OF A SMALL GROUP PROJECT

Divide the class into teams. Each member of a team chooses one of the reading assignments (Selections A, B, C, D, and E). Provide time for each "assignment alike" group to meet, read the selection, and discuss its main ideas. Then have the teams get together, and each team presents the material to the others, using the ideas from the reading selection. Finally, bring all the teams together to review key ideas, terms, or operations. In a block-scheduled class, the daily agenda might look like this:

15 minutes	Attendance, introduction to the process, organization of teams, distribution of readings
30 minutes	Students meet in assignment alike groups ("expert" groups) to read and discuss key ideas, facts, principles, etc.
30 minutes	Students meet in their teams to review each section. Each member teaches the others the key idea from his/her reading selection.
15 minutes	The teacher convenes the whole class to review and reinforce main ideas, and to give the homework assignment, which builds on the reading and discussion.

With what units/topics/issues might small group work be appropriate in my subject area?

_____

_____

_____

_____

_____

_____

_____

_____

_____

_____

DESIGNING LESSONS

CHAPTER 6

A good lesson will exhibit the characteristics that capture what we know about how students learn. Active approaches can set the stage for powerful learning experiences. Such lessons increase the likelihood that students will make important connections between and among subject matter, and will be more motivated to learn.

WHAT DOES A GOOD LESSON LOOK LIKE?

A good lesson builds on and validates students' prior knowledge. The teacher takes time to find out what students already know, what they want to know, and what skills they feel they need to work on to achieve their own learning goals. (K-W-L [page 48] is one tool you can use to work with prior knowledge.)

A good lesson permits students to make choices and set individual goals as they learn to take responsibility for their own learning.

A good lesson helps students construct accurate understandings and working models of concepts and principles important in a discipline. Where possible, it helps them make connections among disciplines.

A good lesson lets students communicate information in a variety of ways—written, spoken, enacted, danced, displayed, etc.—to ensure that the different ways that students learn are accommodated.

A good lesson engages students and teachers in a dialogue that evokes more than one-word, one-right answers to reinforce the need to think deeply and critically.

A good lesson requires that students use higher order thinking skills such as comparing, contrasting, inferring, and evaluating knowledge as well as recalling, comprehending, and applying information.

A good lesson incorporates and acknowledges students' cultural and linguistic backgrounds through recognizing the value of prior knowledge and student experiences, and by using materials that draw on a variety of cultures and histories.

A good lesson values female students and their work as much as male students and deals with all students equitably.

A good lesson involves students in exploring concepts and skills through a variety of planned learning activities. Such activities may include individual and whole class learning, small group projects, problem-solving tasks, learning stations, role plays and simulations, research reports and oral presentations, cooperative study groups, peer tutoring, community service projects, field trips, learning contracts, and other tasks that provide practice in reading, writing, speaking, and listening.

A good lesson encourages practice in question generation, problem-solving, rehearsal for performances, and product development. It is impractical in many situations to expect students to be able to get together for practice or to complete projects outside of class time. It is a legitimate use of class time to have students work on their projects and products because products and projects afford students time to learn and demonstrate their knowledge and practice skills. Such work also provides you with opportunities to exercise your roles as coach, mentor, and assessor of group and individual work.

A good lesson employs technology as a tool for communicating information and as a tool for gathering, using, and managing information—if a particular technology is deemed to be the best way to teach or demonstrate or practice a certain piece of knowledge or skill. Technology should not be used simply because, like Mount Everest, it is there.

A good lesson allows students to do tasks required in the workplace. This is not to say that education should be used only in the service of getting a job, but memorizing pages of data does not help one get a job or live a better life. Learning how to work with others to investigate an ethical problem posed in a literary work provides students with experiences in teamwork and critical thinking that will prepare them for the world of work and sharpen their own moral senses and possibly their appreciation of the value of literature to mirror the human condition.

A good lesson enables students to learn through multiple intelligences and discover their individual learning preferences.

NEED FOR VARIETY

Just as 90 minutes of lecture would be boring so would 90 minutes of learning stations or workshops or student dialogues day after day. It is important to present students with a variety of activities during the 90 minutes—or whatever length your class periods are. Chapters 3 and 4 have provided a variety of short and longer-term strategy ideas. The question is how to put them together to create an effective daily lesson plan.

In *Teaching in the Block: Strategies for Engaging Active Learners,* Robert Lynn Canady and Michael Rettig suggest breaking down a 95-minute period into one segment of 18 to 25 minutes to state lesson objectives and present new material and then three review segments of 5 minutes that alternate with three guided practice segments of 5 minutes each. The final two segments are 15 to 20 minutes of independent practice and 5 to 10 minutes of review. The lesson begins with a 5- to 10-minute review of the previous day's lesson. This seems to us to move students too frequently from activity to activity, although it may be the most appropriate format for learning and practicing a discrete activity such as a math algorithm.

Consider a lesson plan that begins with a 10-minute review of the previous day's lesson and homework and then moves into a 25-minute presentation of new objectives and material. The next 30 minutes are used for an activity that has students working with that material. Reteaching takes place in the next 15 minutes, and the final 10 minutes are used to bring closure to the day. This format provides a longer time for students to process the new material and work in groups on a substantive task.

Even here it is useful to provide variety from day to day so that your lesson plans do not become so predictable that students can tell you when you'll switch from presentation material to having them move their chairs into circles for small group work.

This chapter provides a variety of lesson plan samples as well as templates and outlines to help you in developing lessons appropriate for block-of-time scheduling.

Some activities for reviewing homework assignments:
Turn to Your Neighbor and . . . (p. 37)
Inside-Outside Circles (p. 51)
Pairs Check (p. 54)
Roundtable (p. 55)
Think-Pair-Share (p. 45)
Send a Problem (p. 56)

Some activities for closure:
Ticket to Leave (p. 39)
How Are We Doing? (p. 61)
Summing Up (p. 62)

BLOCK SCHEDULE—SAMPLE LESSON 1

20-25 min. Teach criteria for:
- Oral performance
- Written performance
- Behavior

30 min. Prepare presentation in teams of 2 or 3.

30 min. Groups practice for oral performance or peer editing for written performance. (Groups need to be ready to present by next class period.)

5 min. Closure on the learning activity.

Group processing. Each person within each group tells what the group did well.

Adapted from: Bena Kallick, Education Consultant.

BLOCK SCHEDULE—SAMPLE LESSON 2

10 min. Review of "Ticket to Leave" questions from previous day.

15 min. Review of homework assignment using "Pairs Check."

60 min. Learning Stations

10 min. • Establish objectives, tasks, timetable (the activity will last for five days).
• Teams rotate every 25 minutes.

5 min. Closure: Review process and objectives for learning stations.

Assign work on learning station notes in preparation for final report; textbook reading, pages xx-xx.

BLOCK SCHEDULE—SAMPLE LESSON 3

5 min. Review homework.

10 min. Review learning from previous day by writing similar problems on the board.

15 min. Students practice by completing worksheets.

10 min. Introduce new learning.

30 min. Students practice new learning in groups.

10 min. Reconvene whole group to reteach new learning.

5 min. Assign problems from text as homework.

5 min. Students write in their journals new problem solution.

DESIGNING ACTUAL LESSONS

Review each of the sample lesson plans on this page. Think about how each would work with your subject matter. How would you revise each one to make it work for your courses?

_____
_____
_____
_____
_____
_____

BLOCK SCHEDULE—SAMPLE LESSON 4

10 min.	As students enter the room, message on overhead reads, "In teams of two, you have 10 min. to review _____ from yesterday."
5-10 min.	Quiz Display answers on overhead for quick check.
15 min.	Whole class instruction (new learning).
10 min.	Students actively process new learning in teams of two.
15 min.	Whole class instruction (more new learning).
10 min.	Students actively process new learning in teams of two.
15 min.	Bring learning to whole group; how to solve problem, explain, discuss, demonstrate.
5 min.	Closure on the learning activity. Assign homework on new as well as old learning.

Adapted from: Bena Kallick, Education Consultant.

BLOCK SCHEDULE—SAMPLE LESSON 5

5-10 min.	Students check homework in pairs.
5-10 min.	Teacher discusses homework assignment.
15 min.	Whole class instruction (new learning).
5 min.	Students brainstorm in groups of three.
20 min.	Problem-solving activity.
15 min.	Whole group shares.
20 min.	Formal write-up: lab, essay, procedure.
5 min.	Closure on the learning activity. Group processing. Each person within each group tells what the group did well.

Adapted from: Bena Kallick, Education Consultant.

DESIGNING ACTUAL LESSONS

Review each of the sample lesson plans on this page. Think about how each would work with your subject matter. How would you revise each one to make it work for your courses?

_____
_____
_____
_____
_____

BLOCK SCHEDULE—SAMPLE LESSON 6

Block Schedule—Sample Lesson 7

DESIGNING ACTUAL LESSONS

The sample lessons on this page illustrate graphically how a block of time can be organized. If you were using these formats with your classes, how much time would you assign to each segment?

_____

_____

_____

_____

_____

_____

Block Schedule—Sample Lesson 8

Adapted from: Gary W. Kinsey. Workshop Handouts, "Block Scheduling: The Whys, Hows, and What to Dos." The Center for Professional Development and Resources.

BLOCK SCHEDULE—SAMPLE LESSON 9

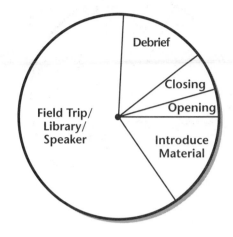

Block Schedule—Sample Lesson 10

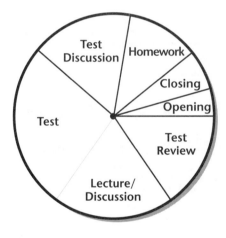

Adapted from: Gary W. Kinsey. (1996) Workshop Handouts, "Block Scheduling: The Whys, Hows, and What to Dos." The Center for Professional Development and Resources.

DESIGNING ACTUAL LESSONS

The sample lessons on this page illustrate graphically how a block of time can be organized. If you were using these formats with your classes, how much time would you assign to each segment?

_____
_____
_____
_____
_____
_____

EIGHT QUESTIONS FOR PLANNING LESSONS IN THE BLOCK

Before you begin to develop your lesson, ask yourself the following questions to help you focus on the content, skills, and students for whom you are designing the lesson.

1. In setting up this lesson, what can I do to develop a positive learning climate, one that demonstrates acceptance, comfort, and order?

_____

_____

_____

2. What can I do to make the learning tasks clear? How will I help students to feel confident that they can do the work I will require of them?

_____

_____

_____

3. What is the focus of this lesson? Will it require students to acquire new information, practice a skill, or both?
   • If they will acquire new information, how will I have them report out or show me what they have learned or understood?
   • If they will practice a new skill, how will they get feedback?

_____

_____

_____

4. What strategies will I use to help students make meaning, organize information, or store/retrieve these ideas? How can I help students connect concepts and big ideas?

_____

_____

_____

5. What models or steps will I present? How can the skills to be mastered be demonstrated? How much practice and application will be necessary? How will students use this skill in life?

_____

_____

_____

6. How can I build in opportunities for generating new knowledge and using divergent thinking?

_____

_____

_____

7. How will I "chunk" the content so that there is a good balance between presentation and interaction?

_____

_____

_____

8. At what points in the lesson will I build in time for students to reflect on, summarize, and reinforce what they have learned? How will I bring this period to closure?

_____

_____

_____

Adapted from: Cerylle C. Moffett, Education Consultant.

A DAILY LESSON
PLANNING FRAMEWORK

Think about a lesson you are planning to teach. Make a few notes to yourself about some of the key choices you must make in designing your lesson, and the approximate amount of time you will spend on each segment.

PREPLANNING

1. Major Learning Objectives: (Relate the content and skills to national, state or local curriculum standards or frameworks.)

_____

_____

_____

_____

_____

_____

_____

2. Specific Content or Skills to Be Introduced: (List key terms, concepts, etc.)

_____

_____

_____

_____

_____

_____

_____

_____

3. Materials and Other Resources Required: (List books, manuals, media, equipment, speakers, or other supplies to have on hand for this lesson.)

_____

_____

_____

_____

_____

_____

_____

_____

4. Assessment: (Indicate how students will demonstrate learning in class; how you will monitor and document progress, i.e., observation checklists, videotapes, self-assessments, products, or performances.)

_____

_____

_____

_____

_____

_____

_____

_____

REAL-TIME CHOREOGRAPHY

1. _____ minutes   Opening Strategy: (Review, overview, motivation, focus, use of prior knowledge, discussion of homework.)

2. _____ minutes   Introduction of New Knowledge or Skill: (Indicate how students will access the new information, i.e., lecture, demonstration, directed reading, videotape.)

3. _____ minutes   Transitional Activities: (Short interactive or reflective opportunities, regrouping strategies, or opportunities for movement.)

4. _____ minutes   Opportunity for Application and Use of Knowledge: (Hands-on activities, small group projects, problems, role play, laboratory experiments, learning centers.)

5. _____ minutes   Assignment for Next Time: (Write as directions to post for students.)

6. _____ minutes   Closing Strategies: (Summaries, reflections, journal writing, report-outs, status reports.)

AN ELEVEN-POINT
LESSON PLAN REVIEW

Review each lesson plan as you develop it, and assign one point for each of the following design features. This lesson:

1. is based on a defined curriculum standard or learner goal. _____

2. is focused on understanding a problem, dilemma, or question. _____

3. includes three different kinds of learning activities: an initial activity, a core learning experience, and a culminating activity. _____

4. provides time for students to practice skills or to apply/process information. _____

5. introduces or illustrates specific thinking tools or strategies. _____

6. engages students in metacognition (awareness of their own thinking processes) or reflection (analysis of their own learner progress). _____

7. helps students make connections to other subjects or their personal lives. _____

8. includes specific steps by which I will be able to evaluate students' levels of understanding or mastery of specific skills. _____

9. provides opportunities for students to work in different grouping structures. _____

10. incorporates appropriate technologies for locating, accessing, processing, manipulating, or presenting information. _____

11. provides opportunities for students to move. _____

TOTAL _____

NEXT STEPS TO IMPLEMENTING INSTRUCTION IN THE BLOCK

What can you do personally to turn all these strategies, tools, and tips into reality?

___ **Read.** Read as much as you can about block scheduling and instructional strategies in general and read over time. Don't stop at the end of the first year or the second. Professional development is continuous development.

___ **Renew.** Renew your energy and your enthusiasm. Take a course, go to educational conferences and conventions, sign up for voluntary in-services that your district offers, attend one-day workshops or seminars on topics of interest to you that commercial companies give.

___ **Talk.** Talk with other teachers about how they are organizing their learning activities. Talk in the teachers' room, before school, at lunch, after school. Make a date to use planning time to work with another teacher on lessons even if you aren't teamed.

___ **Visit.** Visit other schools with block-of-time schedules and observe classes. Ask the teachers what they think of block scheduling and find out what kinds of new instructional practices they've instituted. Ask the administrators what they think, and don't forget to ask the students. Getting lost in the hallways is always a good way to see what's really happening.

___ **Rethink.** Rethink how you view your role as a teacher and your students' role as learner. Once you see yourself as coach and facilitator and your students as responsible for their own learning, you will find it easier to stop worrying about "covering" everything. Learning will become a shared process with your students.

___ **Realign.** Review and realign your curriculum with the essential skills and competencies needed for life in the 21st century. Write new goals and objectives.

___ **Redesign.** Once you have established the differences between the way you taught your previous curriculum and the demands of block scheduling, you will need to redesign your courses to include more technology, more problem solving, and more group work. Remember that assessment needs to be built into instruction and needs to be more performance- and product-based to match your new strategies.

___ **Prepare.** Now that your courses are redesigned, you will need to prepare new sets of activities, learning materials, and investigations to match that curriculum. Do you have to throw out all the materials you have and start all over again? Yes and no. Some of the topics and ideas will certainly work, but you will need to review each piece carefully to make sure that it matches your new strategies. Some items may require a little reworking, but many probably won't work in the new learning environment.

___ **Plan.** Accountability is very important these days. Plan action steps and activities to document the growth of your students over time. Projects and performances are two ways that lend themselves to showing student achievement. Consider also developing observation checklists.

___ **Follow Through.** A new practice may have to be repeated 20 to 30 times before it becomes unconscious and automatic. Don't become discouraged if you or your students forget classroom routines and procedures or if you revert to lecturing rather than coaching. This takes time, and that's what block scheduling is all about.

CHAPTER 7

FREQUENTLY ASKED QUESTIONS ABOUT BLOCK SCHEDULES

The move to block scheduling is a major shift in the structure of a school. It begins with changes in how many times students and teachers meet, and this creates changes in the schedules for sports, band, and Advanced Placement courses. Study halls may be eliminated. Then the culture of the classroom changes as teachers use new instructional strategies that ask students to be active participants in their own learning.

For those facing the move to block scheduling, such reports of massive change only serve to raise the level of anxiety about how to teach in the block. The following are answers to questions we are frequently asked about block scheduling.

UNDERLYING PHILOSOPHY

- **Why are we talking about going to a block schedule?**
  Schools that have chosen to move from a seven- or eight-period-a-day schedule to a block-of-time schedule (four-period-a-day semester schedule, alternating day, or hybrid model) say it increases the time that students spend in quality learning situations, encourages more variety in daily experiences, allows more in-depth and hands-on exploration, improves school climate, reduces disciplinary problems, and better accommodates individual learning needs. Some schedules allow both teachers and students to focus on fewer subjects at once.

  Global changes and changes in our national economy mean that students need to be better prepared than ever for the world of work, continuing education or job training, and for life. Schools that consider changing to a block schedule are often concerned about more effectively equipping students for the challenges they will face.

- **What are the instructional benefits to longer blocks of time?**

  Among the instructional benefits are more opportunities for students to develop higher order thinking, explore knowledge in depth, have substantive conversations, make connections to issues beyond the classroom, acquire research and organizational skills, cultivate problem-solving abilities, demonstrate effective communication, and demonstrate knowledge through use. "Regular" schedules promote quick answer and recall rather than in-depth knowledge.

- **Will more classroom time be allotted for hands-on lessons and less lecture?**

  A well-ordered teacher explanation or teacher-directed lesson can be good for learners. A steady diet of it every day in every class gets, well, boring. The same would be true for more active learning strategies like cooperative learning, projects, computer software. Pacing, variety, and engagement are the keys to success in block-of-time teaching.

- **How does the time we'll be spending in a block of time compare with the time we currently spend on academics within our state guidelines?**

  It's not about time; it's about learning. It's not really about scheduling; it's about classroom change. At Champlin Park High School in Champlin, Minnesota, the charge to the School Scheduling Committee was stated this way:

  1. How can we divide our school day in a way that better supports our school goals and course objectives?

  2. How can we divide our school day in a way to enhance student opportunities to take more courses?

  3. How can we divide our school day in a way that reduces class size and provides other benefits to teachers and students?

  4. How can we devise a flexible scheduling option to permit remediation or enrichment time for students to work with staff?

  5. How can we alter our yearly calendar in ways to provide better instruction?

  6. Do we have any contractual issues that will need to be addressed as a result of a different daily schedule or school year calendar?

- **Is there a down side to block scheduling?**

  There's probably a down side to anything. The question is, do the benefits (to students, to teachers, to the school in general, to the community) that are possible because of the block outweigh the liabilities? That's the key. "What is in the best interests of OUR students?"

The Up Side

- A 90-minute period allows teachers to develop fully key concepts and encourages use of active learning instructional strategies. It gets students beyond "recall."
- After teachers have introduced a new skill, students have more time to practice that skill, and teachers can be more certain that students are applying it correctly.
- More active learning instructional strategies accommodate a wider variety of learning styles.
- Students have only four classes to prepare for each day.
- Less time is lost moving from one class to another during the day.
- Tardiness is generally reduced.
- Block scheduling allows more time for use of technology.
- Block scheduling is more beneficial to at-risk students than traditional scheduling.

The Down Side

- Block scheduling represents a change in the daily routine for many veteran teachers.
- Students may require additional coaching and direct instruction in study habits and organizational techniques, especially as research projects and problem-based assignments increase.
- Teachers will invest more time in estimating, sequencing, and planning in the first few years of block scheduling.
- Additional staff development time may be required to assist teachers in adapting instructional techniques to a longer block of time.
- Additional time may be needed to review school policy, student handbooks, etc., to ensure that they are "in line" with the new schedule. Time may need to be spent to modify them to reflect the new schedule, for example, attendance policy, tardiness policy, "no school days," etc.

- Block-scheduled classrooms may require new materials and activities to supplement the lecture as the primary means of instruction.
- Block-scheduled classrooms require a broader range of assessment strategies than many teachers presently use, for example, projects, performances, products, portfolios, peer reviews, and personal conferences.
- Block-scheduled classrooms require a broader range of grouping strategies than many teachers presently employ in their classrooms.
- Some teachers may decide that they cannot or will not adapt to this kind of teaching and may choose to seek employment in a more traditional setting. This may result in a sense of loss in a faculty that has enjoyed continuity and cohesiveness in the past.
- Students who are absent, especially those with an established attendance problem, will be missing even more class time than in the traditional bell schedule
- Additional staff and classroom space may be required to accommodate some block scheduling options.

- **Is there a problem at our school that block scheduling will solve?**
  Are you engaging in change because you perceive there is a problem, or because you see this as an opportunity to explore how students can be involved in a wider variety of learning experiences? Schools that have chosen to pursue a block schedule view block scheduling as a means of:
  - increasing options for students to take more courses in a year.
  - improving the quality of learning through more productive time on task.
  - promoting student success through fewer classes at one time.
  - decreasing interruptions to instruction during the day.
  - creating more positive relationships between students and teachers, and helping students feel more connected to school.
  - reducing the number of students that teachers have during a semester so teachers can get to better know the students they do have.

Block scheduling is not a panacea.

PRACTICAL ISSUES

- **What about study halls?**
  Most schools moving to block scheduling are eliminating study halls. Some schools, such as Seward High School, Seward, Nebraska, provide a 30-minute "guided" study for 9th and 10th grade students.

- **If block scheduling eliminates study halls, how and when will students be pulled out for services such as guidance appointments, Academic Support Center, remediation for failing the state competency test, and so on?**
  There is no one best way to do any of these things. Whatever your decision, if you go to block-of-time learning, it probably won't be the same as when you were on the traditional bell schedule. Otherwise, it wouldn't be a change. In some schools, guidance staff work the lunch rooms as a way of increasing contact with students without pulling them from class. The role of the Academic Support Center may change to provide more counseling, tutoring, placement and preparation of transfer students who have not been in the block before. In other schools, a separate "seminar block" or a long block of time in the middle of the day, built around lunch, is used for tutoring, work on projects, library research, test preparation, computer laboratory, etc.

  At Robinson High School in Robinson, Illinois, the 4 x 4 block schedule includes four 81-minute classes per semester, a daily activity period (three different lengths and times on a rotating cycle), three lunch periods of 40 minutes each (29 minutes for band students), band rehearsal from 11:20-12:05 daily on an all-year basis, and 4 minutes hallway passing time between classes.

- **Will this eliminate field trips?**
  Most schools with block schedules encourage teachers to plan integrated or combined course field trips to reduce the impact on students who would otherwise miss other classes. It might be a stretch to combine small engine repair and food services field trips but there are many natural overlaps that maximize the opportunity to learn while not negatively impacting other classes.

  Some schools worry about the transportation costs that field trips represent. Using your own school campus creatively can provide the solution in some subject areas. Science courses could establish a nature trail or use the environment surrounding the school for research projects. A block schedule allows for greater use of outside resources and represents a way to bring the community into the classroom.

- **Does a 90-minute block cut time spent on a particular subject?**

  The block forces teachers to decide what is most important. Again, this is not about time, but about learning. A home economics teacher at Asheboro High School in Asheboro, North Carolina, said after the first full year on the 4 x 4 block: "State guidelines say that I must teach both international foods and egg preparation. I can't cover both in our concentrated curriculum, semester schedule. So we do a unit on 'international eggs'."

  You'll "cover" less, but what does that mean? Perfect transmission does not guarantee perfect reception. Your students will probably understand and demonstrate more of the knowledge and skills of the course by using active learning strategies.

  A few more highlights from the research that has been conducted to date:

  - Student retention of material is as good or better than in a traditional schedule.

  - Student attention during long periods is as good or better than in a traditional schedule.

  - Student cognition is as good or better than in a traditional schedule. (Activities permit more higher-order thinking.)

  - Student behavior is as good or better than in a traditional schedule.

  - Student attitudes toward learning and the school community increase compared to a traditional schedule.

- **How will the curriculum be affected by block scheduling?**

  If, by curriculum, you mean the selection of textbooks, workbooks, and manuals, you will probably choose ones that feature more small group activities and real-world investigations. If, by curriculum, you mean the number of chapters or units of study you complete in your course, you will probably "cover" fewer of them but what your students DO know will stay with them longer and better. If, by curriculum, you mean a set of experiences you believe are vital to your discipline, you will probably spend more time asking yourself (and your students) if they are mastering the essential skills and concepts you and your colleagues have agreed upon. Here, your work on your state and local curriculum frameworks and the content standards for your discipline will hold you in good stead.

  See Chapter 2, "Adapting Your Curriculum to Block-of-Time Scheduling."

As a result of introducing a "flexible block" schedule at Northwest High School in Grand Island, Nebraska, that requires teachers to work in interdisciplinary teams, teachers reported:

- We are more responsive to student needs. (89%)
- I am getting to know my students better. (89%)
- I am doing things instructionally that I would not have tried a year ago. (89%)

See Chapter 4, "'Blocking'" Lessons: A Classroom Choreography."

- **How should we plan for longer (90-100 minute) class periods? How many different types of activities should we include?**

  There is no one right way or single formula for blocking out effective use of time. It can vary by subject. This is where each teacher's professional knowledge, repertoire of skills, and ability to match strategies to student needs come in to play. At least three different kinds of activities are recommended during a block period as a rough guideline for planning. Many lessons in block schedules include teacher presentation (explanation) followed by small group work (processing and application) concluded by a wrap-up, summary, report, or review (synthesis).

- **Would a teacher be able to accomplish a whole curriculum in half a year?**

  Probably not. Most teachers in a block-of-time schedule say they don't "cover" all of the same modules, lessons, or chapters they did under the old schedule, but they say that their students know more and can actually do more.

- **Should math and science teachers expect to cover as much material as they would in two regular length periods of two days?**

  If by "cover" you mean, can you personally "go over" or "say" the words, concepts, or skills that form the syllabus of your course as it is configured for 45-minute classes, the answer is probably no. A block lesson is not just two 45-minute lessons stuck together. Teachers who have "been there" generally report that they "cover" fewer chapters, but that the real knowledge and demonstrated competencies their students acquire are longer lasting and more relevant. This is not just a scheduling issue. It is a curriculum issue. Statewide curriculum standards are also influencing "what is taught."

- **How would math class be handled in the block situation?**
  This a tough one, no doubt about it. Our math curriculum crams more stuff in than many other countries, including ones that outscore us on standardized tests. Some math teachers in block-scheduled math classes say that they can teach two or three related concepts in one math block, thereby saving time. Others try to teach two unrelated or only slightly related lessons in one period, using the same delivery style for both. (The "I'm going to do what I have always done" approach.) Most math teachers say they try to provide some time for group problem solving or individual application during some part of the block.

  Some solutions for math courses that have been proposed include eliminating the overlaps and repetition between courses (such as Algebra I and II), teaching them sequentially, and combining the courses into a new configuration (Algebra A, B, and C).

See Appendix A, "Checklist of Action Steps for Teaching in a Block-Scheduled Classroom," to help you put into the practice the tips and tools in this chapter.

- **What is your experience with schools who have taken longer blocks of time and split the block to accommodate minor classes?**
  The process has worked more effectively where teachers have created new elective courses to be offered as singletons. This creates more options and choices for students. The process has worked less effectively when, say, a math teacher and a science teacher agree to a math block and a science block scheduled at the same time, then the math teacher takes half of the students and teaches them math for 45 minutes while the science teacher teaches the other half science. At the break, they switch groups. This does not provide extended opportunity to learn, does not provide the students with new choices and options, does not encourage new curriculum materials, teaching strategies, or student assessments. It just "masks" the status quo.

- **Shop teachers have always taught a double period. How would the new block affect shop classes?**
  Any teacher who refers to his/her classroom as "shop," "kitchen," "laboratory," "studio," "stage," "gym," or "garage," is probably wondering what all the fuss about block scheduling is about. These teachers have been organizing and managing their courses around active learning cycles and performance-based assessments for years. At the same time, there may be some "new tricks" for them to learn, too, particularly in areas of interactive strategies to sustain thinking, curriculum compacting, and content integration.

See Chapter 3, "Short Takes," for some practical suggestions.

- **Should we use the beginning of each class for some type of review?**

  If appropriate, yes. The opening activity should be short, however, only enough time to reinforce, review, focus, get settled. It should not eat into the main activities for the day.

- **What about special needs students? Do schools generally use half of a period so that special needs teachers continue to see their most in-need students each day?**

  Practices vary. Many schools are moving toward instructional models where the resource (specialist) teacher works in the room along with the regular (generalist) teacher, but in a co-teaching context. Students are organized into different groupings within the class on a regular basis. The resource teacher does not work only or exclusively with students with special needs. The resource teacher is not an instructional assistant, but an equal partner in the daily planning process. The book Inclusion: 450 Strategies for Success (Peggy A. Hammekan, Peytral Publications, Minnetonka, Minnesota, 1995) includes strategies for modifying curriculum and other practical planning forms, for setting up inclusionary programs.

- **How do teachers generally deal with testing? Do they give longer tests or only use part of the period?**

  First, don't let the kids con you into giving them 90 minutes to take a 45-minute test. Block scheduling is not about time, it is about learning. Maximize that learning time on a test day by:
  - using part of the time for focused review or test preparation in small groups
  - giving the test (paper and pencil) but including some open-ended questions or performance-based items, then
  - collecting the test and reviewing some of the most challenging questions, describing the components of exemplary responses, having students write in learning logs or journals, etc.

  You can also use the entire period by having students complete three test components:
  - a paper-and-pencil portion of short answer/multiple choice items
  - an open-ended problem-solving/essay/performance-based portion and
  - a self-assessment/goal setting/journal entry form.

- **Do teachers generally find that reviewing on the day of a test is a good idea?**
  Reviewing on the day of the test can be a good idea if it is not the only day of review or preparation and if the review activity you assign is focused, novel, and introduces a new skill or perspective. See the article "Creating Tests That Are Worth Taking," by Grant Wiggins, Educational Leadership (Volume 49, Number 8, pp. 26-33, May, 1992).

- **What will the effect of 4 x 4 block scheduling be on our students?**

  ## IMPACT ON STUDENTS

  There are a variety of answers to this question.
  - Under an 8-credit schedule, a student can earn up to 32 credits a year. This may require a change in the number of credits required for graduation in some districts.
  - Overall class size generally decreases slightly, say from 24.4 to 21.5. Some classes, i.e., writing, may be reduced even more. This provides more opportunity for coaching, conferencing, and small group projects/activities.
  - Levels of stress reported by students generally decrease. The school climate becomes more relaxed. Tardiness and disciplinary referrals decrease.
  - Mathematics and foreign language skills are not severely impaired by gaps in sequential courses.
  - Enrollments in elective subjects increase (20% is common).
  - The number of students failing in one or more classes decreases.
  - The number of students earning honor roll recognition increases (14% is common).

  What students at Dickinson High School in Dickinson, North Dakota, said:
  - "You can get more credits."
  - "My grades are better than last year."
  - "You can learn more."
  - "Less homework to do each night"
  - "More time to get organized between class"
  - "More time to really understand things"
  - "Time to finish labs that would have taken two days"
  - "Miss fewer classes for extra-curricular activities"
  - "More time to do different things in class"

Other positive features associated with block schedule include:

- Calmer atmosphere in hallway
- Increased attention and seriousness of purpose on the part of students
- Time for out-of-building activities
- Teachers get to know students better.
- Students use library/media center for research.
- More individualized instruction
- Fewer absences

- **Will break time be incorporated for students?**

  Breaks within the block may not be needed if there is a good flow and variety of activities to engage students. Breaks may be given at the teacher's discretion if there is a need for set-up or transition, but this practice should not be abused or it will defeat the primary purpose of the block. Some teachers issue a set number of "mini" hall passes that allow students to go to the bathroom, if needed. If the passes are not used by the end of the term, they can be turned in for bonus points.

  Movement needs to be built into classroom routines. After 37 minutes of work on an activity, students should have at least 90 seconds in which to move around. This kind of movement is energizing, rather than disruptive, if carefully planned.

  In addition, passing time between periods may increase to ten minutes. Passing bells may be eliminated.

- **Should students start homework at the end of the period?**

  Sometimes, especially when the concept or skill they will apply is complex or difficult. You don't want them going home to practice doing it wrong. "Unlearning" can be more difficult than learning it right the first time.

  As a general rule, we advise against using too much time on independent practice, unless your course is based on project work, self-contained learning activity packages, or multi-grade levels. There are so many other more powerful learning experiences that can take place between students and between teachers and students. There is a difference between guided practice (students working on a specific skill while the teacher monitors and coaches) and "getting started on your homework early."

- **If we meet every day for five days is there sufficient time inbetween for students to read and work with the material?**

  In most block schedules, both teachers and students have fewer courses each semester. That means homework assignments can be longer or more complex and comprehensive, but teachers need to grade and return assigned work more promptly.

- **Will homework increase?**

  Teachers may or may not assign more homework under the 4 x 4 plan. Assignments might be more comprehensive and complex, but students have fewer classes to prepare for each day. Rather than having homework in six or seven classes, students may have homework in three or four. In a block-scheduled classroom, students also have more time to ask questions about the homework assignment before leaving class.

- **Isn't make-up work a concern if a student misses two days of classes and thus is almost a week behind?**

  It is the student who bears the responsibility. Teachers in the block schedule may assign study buddies whose job it is to inform each other of missed assignments and to help each other catch up.

  In other classrooms, students are expected to work in teams. Each team keeps a notebook containing homework and in-class assignments. The team manager places the information in the notebook, and the whole team helps "catch up" the absent student. This assumes that every class is not a full lecture class, so students have some time to work together on new assignments or on review assignments.

  Some schools have instituted Academic Support Centers where students can go to get computer tutorials or in-person assistance from teachers or students. Nashoba Regional High School in Bolton, Massachusetts, is one such school.

  Many teachers find it easier, not harder, for students to get caught up in the block model. Teachers find there is more time to meet with a student during the longer class period.

- **Will this schedule restrict students who transfer in?**

  It shouldn't. Some schools with block schedules provide an assistance or support center where students can go to get special tutoring or be brought up to speed if they have transferred in from schools with shorter periods. As more schools move to the block, this should become less of a concern.

- **If a student is failing or doing poorly in a block-scheduled course, how should this be handled?**

  In some schools, a regular "semester" grade is issued after 9 weeks. At the same time, D-F grades may be reported weekly, with a phone call being made to parents whose son or daughter has a D or F in one or more classes. Having fewer students and fewer classes allows earlier detection and earlier intervention with student problems.

  A student who can be identified by the end of the quarter can be removed from the course and placed in an elective. At the start of the new semester, the student can enroll in the previously failed course. One way to look at it is that if you are failing in October, you can start over again with a fresh start in January. Under the full year, shorter period schedule, you stay failing until June, unless you improve dramatically or drop out first. Which is better?

- **How will we provide information for students so that they understand the reasons for change?**

  The school scheduling committee may want to spell out some of the consequences and implications of block scheduling, for example, the increased importance of daily attendance and of keeping up with assignments, the use of a study buddy system, or the establishment of new project- or performance-based test requirements. There may also be less passing-in-the-hall times during the school day and other changes in routines for students they should know about.

- **Is a student survey possible prior to the pilot?**

  It is highly recommended. The block-schedule concept should be described to students at a schoolwide assembly prior to any survey. This will reduce the rumor mill and typical misinformation that goes on in any organization. The same dissemination of information should be done for parents and other community members. I interviewed groups of students in one high school where they told me that their teachers had given them very different opinions (both positive and negative), but little real data on how the proposed schedule would work or what they had read about it. The students were generally in favor of the concept based on its perceived benefits to them, but were skeptical if SOME of their teachers could function effectively in the new design.

  As your representative school steering committee pursues block scheduling, it should use surveys of faculty, students, and parents to determine the level of acceptance of the concept. This will enable your steering committee to make appropriate accommodations. In addition, informational meetings should be held with faculty, students, and the community to discuss issues and concerns such as expanded educational options, increased academic success, the scheduling process, and special programs (band, choir, etc.).

- **What should teachers expect in terms of work in a longer period?**

That depends on the type of block schedule you have agreed upon. In a 4 x 4 or semester schedule, teachers give longer and more complex assignments because students are taking fewer subjects at one time. Classes are much more interactive, with students putting more problems on the board, discussing problems in small groups, and preparing for a course test as a "study team" but taking the test individually. Many teachers are holding students responsible for completing learning tasks outside of the class or laboratory periods, such as reading assignments, learning vocabulary terms, writing critical review papers. Of course, the work must be such that a student can reasonably complete and understand it without a great deal of teacher explanation.

How will your school orient students to the "realities" of the new schedule? Block schedules usually result in students:

- working in small groups
- being responsible for helping and tutoring each other for short segments
- conducting more research assignments
- completing assigned projects outside of class
- learning and applying organizational skills and study habits
- becoming more critical self-assessors of their own products and performances.

- **What caveats exist for teachers? Do teachers tend to cover too much or too little? Do teachers depend too much on discussion over the longer period? Do teachers tend to give too much homework because there is an intervening (alternate-day schedule) day?**

Caveat #1. Don't try to do the new thing using the old way. If you judge your competence by the number of chapters you cover rather than by what your students can actually do and understand, you will probably frustrate yourself. Our curriculums are changing—as a result of international studies, national professional organization initiatives, and state policies and curriculum frameworks. Maybe Algebra 1 should be a two-year program. That's a curriculum question, not a scheduling question.

Caveat #2. It's not either-or; it's and/both.
There will always be room for well-ordered, skillfully delivered explanation. Your students need that. But they also need time to process and apply what you have so skillfully presented, so that the learning sticks, and so that you can see or hear what they have not gotten quite right. The lecture isn't dead; it just isn't the only thing that brings life to a classroom. We must constantly expand our repertoire of teaching techniques.

See Appendix A, "Checklist of Action Steps for Teaching in a Block-Scheduled Classroom," to help you put into the practice the tips and tools in this chapter.

Most teachers conduct recitations, which are different from discussions, in their classes. To use discussion well, teachers must teach the skills of civil discourse and higher level thinking needed so that students learn from the process of conversation. Students need to be able to answer factual questions before they can deal with interpretive questions and before they can handle evaluative questions well. We tend to stop at the level of factual recall.

- *Caveat #3. Be time disciplined.*
  In the beginning, you might worry whether you have enough planned to last a whole 90 minutes. In a short time, you will wonder how you got along on only 45 minutes. Getting the most out of 90 minutes means that you can't talk too much, that you can't let the students talk too much, and that you must constantly be reinforcing and connecting the important ideas and concepts. Group work must include time limits, equal participation, and structured discussion (questions, problems, or writing prompts provided by you, the teacher) to be effective.

- *Caveat #4. Let go.*
  Letting go and giving more responsibility for learning to students can make you feel inadequate. Many teachers say they feel like they are not working if they are not talking, or they fear losing control if they are not standing up and demonstrating something. Many of the newer strategies for organizing classes leave some veteran professionals feeling outdated, inadequate, and somehow "wrong." That's a common emotional reaction to change. It's also not true. You are still designing the lessons and coaching and assessing the students.

- **How are we going to evaluate the effectiveness of the block schedule?**

  The scheduling committee at each school should list the indicators of success it hopes to achieve through the type of block schedule that is chosen. Then the committee should make a plan for monitoring progress and collecting data related to those indicators. Some of the indicators used by other schools that have moved to a block schedule include:

  - improved daily attendance
  - increased number of students achieving honor roll status
  - increased number of students completing courses
  - decreased disciplinary referrals/school suspensions
  - reduced numbers of D, F, and Incomplete grades.

PROFESSIONAL DEVELOPMENT

- **Should we plan workshops for teachers to develop skills for hands-on learning?**

  Yes. Emphasis should be placed on designing lessons that provide good pacing, a variety of learning activities during each block, and plenty of student engagement with materials, problems, and ideas.

- **Should a staff development program provide opportunities to develop sample lesson plans?**

  Yes. A staff development program should provide sample lesson plans, a planning template, and the opportunity to practice lesson design with feedback.

- **Should we visit a school that is already using block scheduling?**

  Yes, and not just to get answers, but to raise questions. How were staff supported during their change process? What did they read, who conducted workshops for them, and what kinds of information helped them with their plans and choices? What do they know now that they wish they knew then? What mistakes did they make and how did they overcome them? Persons who visit other schools should act as investigative reporters, and return with recommendations and findings for their school.

- **Should we implement a plan to train staff for block scheduling, such as in-service, summer workshops (paid), etc.?**

Research and "best practices" suggest that a school considering block scheduling have at least three 2-hour in-service sessions aimed at developing a shared understanding of how block scheduling influences teaching and learning. (Small Group Learning, Lesson Design, Assessment Practices) These sessions should be supplemented by visits to and from other schools, attendance at conferences, and individual preparation.

In the best case scenario, the actual year of implementation is preceded by a 2- or 3-day summer institute during which teachers work on detailed lesson plans for the first ten days of school and a pacing guide (for 4 x 4 block) for their curriculum. Two years of training prior to implementation is a bit long for a senior and savvy staff (unless the real agenda is political, or unless you are bundling block scheduling with teacher advisory periods, home visitations, interdisciplinary teamed instruction, or student portfolio management). A stipend for summer institutes is commendable. When the summer institute is offered on a voluntary basis, sometimes the ones who need it the most don't come.

At Pelham High School in Pelham, New Hampshire, an extensive staff development plan was developed to help teachers learn instructional strategies that make the best use of 90-minute blocks. One strategy is to use half the time for direct instruction and checking for understanding, followed by active student learning through research projects, laboratory experiments, application of knowledge, and more in-depth discussion in small groups.

Other important capacities to develop are providing a variety of classroom activities involving individual work, pairs and partners, small group activities (not year-long assignments), and whole group instruction.

READINESS

- **Are we ready to go to a block schedule?**
  There are many kinds of readiness. First, you must have the will (vision for what the block can achieve). Then, you need the skill (the ability to plan and manage learning in longer periods). Finally, you need the resources (staff, budget, supplies, equipment, space) to do the job. If you have less on any of these than you need, you may get less than smooth implementation. Don't fix blame. Fix the system.

GLOSSARY

Alternate-Day Schedule (also known as A/B, Odd/Even, Day 1/Day 2, Week 1/Week 2)

Teachers and students meet every other day rather than every day. In a 7-hour day (420 minutes) a 6-period model of an alternate-day schedule has blocks of approximately 120 minutes; 8-period models have blocks of approximately 90 minutes; 7-period models have 3 alternating blocks of 100-105 minutes while the additional 45-55 minutes is used for 1 year-long course that meets every day.

Trimester Plan

Students take 2 core courses every 60 days.

4 x 4

Students have the same 4 classes lasting 85–100 minutes each for 90 days. Teachers teach 3 courses a semester. What would be a year-long course in a traditional schedule is completed in one semester.

Modified Block

There are a number of variations. One variation is a 4 x 4 block four days a week and a traditional 7- or 8-period day that allows for electives on Friday. Another variation is 2 block courses and 3 single-period classes each day. The latter last a full year.

RESOURCES

BOOKS

Bellanca, J. *Designing Professional Development for Change*. Palatine, Ill.: IRI/Skylight Publishing, 1995.

Canady, R.L., and Rettig, M.D. *Block Scheduling: A Catalyst for Change in High Schools*. Princeton, N.J.: Eye on Education, Inc., 1995. Probably the most comprehensive resource available today, with detailed treatment of alternate day, 4x4, intensive scheduling, and blended models. An excellent chapter on teaching in the block and designing professional development to prepare staff.

Canady, R.L., and Rettig, M.D., eds. *Teaching in the Block: Strategies for Engaging Active Learners*. Princeton, N.J.: Eye on Education, Inc., 1996. Illustrates models of teaching and other instructional strategies that foster active engagement of students in learning.

Carroll, J.M. *The Copernican Plan: Restructuring the American High School*. Andover, Mass.: Regional Laboratory for Educational Improvement of the Northeast and Islands, 1989. This book has served as an impetus for schedule change in schools around the country. Students in schools that have applied Carroll's model have reported that they learned more and worked harder.

Carroll, J.M. *The Copernican Plan Evaluated: The Evolution of a Revolution*. Andover, Mass.: Regional Laboratory for Educational Im-

provement of the Northeast and Islands, 1994.

Fogarty, R.J. *Think About Block Scheduling*. Palatine, Ill.: IRI/Skylight Publishing, Inc., 1995. An excellent resource for school boards, community members, and other policy makers.

Forte, I., and Schurr, S. *The Definitive Middle School Guide: A Handbook for Success*. Nashville, Tenn.: Incentive Publications, 1993. Includes 10 different model schedules and the nuts and bolts of interdisciplinary teaming, advisory, cooperative learning, assessment.

Kosanovic, G.E. *Retooling the Instructional Day*. Reston, Va.: National Association of Secondary School Principals, 1994. Practical examples of modified traditional schedules, block-of-time schedules, modified block-of-time schedules, and modular schedules.

National Commission on Time and Learning. *Prisoners of Time*. Washington, D.C.: National Commission on Time and Learning, 1994. Summary of research findings on the relationship between time and learning in elementary and secondary education.

Williamson, R. *Scheduling the Middle Level School to Meet Early Adolescent Needs*. Reston, Va.: National Association of Secondary School Principals, 1993. Suggestions for developing a master schedule and examples of flexible block-of-time models.

JOURNAL ARTICLES

Bateson, D.J. "Science Achievement in Semester and All-Year Courses." *Journal of Research in Science Teaching,* March 1990: 233-240.

Brophy, B. 1978. "Semestering and the Teaching-Learning Situation." *Canadian Journal of Education* 3, No. 3 (1978): 47-54.

Buckman, D.C., Beston-King, B., and Ryan, S. 1995. "Block Scheduling: A Means to Improve School Climate." *NASSP Bulletin* 79, No. 571 (1995): 9-18.

Canady, R.L. "Parallel Block Scheduling: A Better Way to Organize a School." *Principal,* January 1990: 34-36.

Canady, R.L., and Rettig, M.D. Summer 1992. "Restructuring Middle Level Schedules to Promote Equal Access." *Schools in the Middle,* Summer 1992: 20-26.

Canady, R.L., and Rettig, M.D. "Unlocking the Lockstep High School Schedule." *Phi Delta Kappan,* December 1993: 310-314.

Carroll, J.M. "The Copernican Plan: Restructuring the American High School." *Phi Delta Kappan,* January 1990: 358-365.

Carroll, J.M. "The Copernican Plan Evaluated: The Evolution of a Revolution." *Phi Delta Kappan,* October 1994: 105-113.

Carroll, J.M. "Organizing Time to Support Learning." *The School Administrator,* March 1994: 26-28, 30-33.

Cawelti, G. "Restructuring Large High Schools to Personalize Learning for All." *ERS Spectrum,* Summer 1993: 17-21.

Cushman, K. "Schedules That Bind." *American Educator,* Summer 1989: 35-39.

Cushman, K. "Scheduling in the Essential School." *Horace 5* (May 1989), Coalition of Essential Schools, Brown University, Providence, R.I. Available from Brown.

Edwards, C.M., Jr. "Restructuring to Improve Student Performance." *NASSP Bulletin,* May 1993: 77-88.

Hackmann, D.G. "Improving School Climate: An Alternating-Day Block Schedule." *Schools in the Middle,* September 1995: 28-33.

Hackmann, D.G. "Ten Guidelines for Implementing Block Scheduling." *Educational Leadership,* November 1995: 24-27.

Hinckley, J. "Blocks, Wheels, and Teams: Building a Middle School Schedule." *Music Educators Journal,* February 1992: 26-30.

Hottenstein, D., and Malatesta, C. "Putting a School in Gear With Intensive Scheduling." *The High School Magazine,* December 1993: 28-29.

Kramer, S.L. "What We Know About Block Scheduling and Its Effects on Math Instruction," Part 1. *NASSP Bulletin,* February 1997: 19-42.

Spear, R.C. "Middle Level Team Scheduling: Appropriate Grouping for Adolescents." *Schools in the Middle,* Fall 1992: 30-34.

Strock, G.E., and Hottenstein, D.S. "The First Year Experience: A High School Restructures Through the Copernican Plan." *The School Administrator,* March 1994: 30-31.

Tanner, B., Canady, R.L., and Rettig, M.D. "Scheduling Time to Maximize Staff Development Opportunities." *Journal of Staff Development,* Fall 1995: 14-19.

Traverso, H.P. "Scheduling: From Micro to Macro." *The Practitioner,* 1994. National Association of Secondary School Principals.

RESEARCH REPORTS

Averett, C.P. "Block Scheduling in North Carolina High Schools." North Carolina Department of Public Instruction, Raleigh, 1994.

Cawelti, G. "High School Restructuring: A National Study." Educational Research Service, Alexandria, Va., 1994.

Cox, L.C. "A Study of the Effects of a Block Scheduling Program With High School Students Who Are At-Risk." Dissertation, University of Houston, 1994.

Eineder, D.V. "The Effects of Block Scheduling in a High School." Dissertation, University of Alabama, 1996.

Guskey, T. R., and Kifer, E. "Evaluation of a High School Block Schedule Restructuring Program." American Educational Research Association, San Francisco, 1995.

Hart, K. "The Intensive Scheduling Model at a Suburban Public High School: Student and Teacher Behavior Changes." Dissertation, Temple University, 1994.

Sturgis, J. "Block Scheduling and Student Achievement." Occasional Paper Series No. 20, University of Maine College of Education, 1995.

VIDEOTAPES

High School Block Scheduling. Presented by Robert Lynn Canady. The Video Journal of Education, 549 West 3560 South, Salt Lake City, UT 84115-4225; (800) 572-1153.

- *Reorganizing Time for Student Achievement* (Program 1, 30 min.)
- *New Opportunities With Block Scheduling* (Program 2, 38 min.)

Educational Impact Associates and NASSP Videotape Series for Middle and High School Educators. Educational Impact Associates, Stefwalt Road, Hatboro, PA 19040; (215) 674-5038; fax (215) 674-2683.

- *Intensive Scheduling: Restructuring Through Time Management* (No. 2, 30 min.)
- *How to Teach in a Longer Block of Time: Retooling the Typical Secondary School Teacher* (No. 3, 30 min.)
- *Intensive Scheduling Revisited: The Restructured High School Two Years Later* (No. 5, 44 min.)
- *Intensive Scheduling: A Teacher's Perspective From Inside the Classroom (Part 1) Featuring Math, Science, Social Studies, English, Foreign Language, Computer Science and Business* (No. 8, 79 min.)
- *Intensive Scheduling: A Teacher's Perspective From Inside the Classroom (Part 2) Featuring Health & Physical Education, Music, Special Education, Art, Family & Consumer Science, and Guidance* (No. 9, 67 min.)
- *Intensive Scheduling: A Parent and Student Perspective* (No. 10, 71 min.)
- *Block Scheduling: A National Perspective* (No. 11, 45 min.)

Using Scheduling and Grading Options to Raise the Achievement of Career-Bound High School Students. Presented by Robert Lynn Canady. (No. 94V11, two-tape set, 180 min.) Southern Regional Education Board, 592 10th Street, NW, Atlanta, GA 30318-5790; (404) 875-9211; fax (404) 872-1477.

Alternative Scheduling. Presented by Robert Lynn Canady and Elliot Merenbloom. Three-tape set comes with facilitator's guide and Canady's 1995 book (see Books). Association for Supervision and Curriculum Development, 1250 North Pitt Street, Alexandria, VA 22314; (800) 933-ASCD or (703) 549-9110; fax (703) 299-8631.

RESOURCES ON THE INTERNET

http://www.classroom.net/classweb/myhome. html Wasson High School offers tips from teachers on planning for block schedule, tips for teaching in the block, the rationale for changing to block schedule, sample lesson plans, and links to other resources on block.

http://k12.oit.umass.edu/block/block.html Mirror site for many of the Wasson High School files.

http://carei.coled.umn.edu/bsmain.htm Resources, research, and hot links related to block scheduling provided by Center for Applied Research and Educational Improvement (CAREI) and the University of Minnesota. CAREI also maintains a listserv for discussions about block schedule.

http://www.citynet.net/putnam/4x4.html Frequently asked questions (and answers) from Putnam County, West Virginia. All high schools in Putnam County are on 4x4 block.

http://www.inmind.com/lhs/wired/education/ block.html Liberty High School (950 students) in Bedford, Virginia, shares teacher survey data related to their block scheduling program.

http://curry.edschool.virginia.edu/~dhv3v/block /BSintro.html Discussion of block scheduling as a means to restructuring secondary schools.

http://www.internet-high.com/4x4/ The pro's and con's of block scheduling.

http://www.palmbeach.k12.fl.us/9058/blksched. html Includes a pre-implementation checklist and staff development suggestions.

http://www.ed.gov/pubs/studies.html On-line reports from the National Education Commission on Time and Learning include *Prisoners of Time* and its supplementary volumes *Schools and Programs Making Time Work for Students and Teachers* and *Research: What We Know and What We Need to Know.*

http://ericir.syr.edu/Virtual/InfoGuides An invaluable resource including a full text ERIC Digest.

APPENDIX A

CHECKLIST OF ACTION STEPS FOR TEACHING IN A BLOCK-SCHEDULED CLASSROOM

Category A: Background Reading and Preparation

___ 1. I have read some books or articles describing teaching practices appropriate for teaching in extended periods of learning.

___ 2. I have identified some key learning products and academic performances through which students can exhibit their developing skills and knowledge in my course(s). Examples: an insect collection, a community survey, analysis of a controversial issue, design of a mousetrap-powered vehicle, interpretation of an artifact.

___ 3. I have made a personal commitment to organize my course around the "curriculum strands" or topics suggested by my state's Department of Education for my teaching area(s).

___ 4. I have made a personal commitment to become more knowledgeable about using active learning strategies in my subject area: cooperative learning, project-based assignments, problem-based curriculum, using technology, responding to individual learner differences, multiple intelligences, conducting class discussions.

___ 5. I have made a personal commitment to use one or more alternative assessment practices: product assessment, performance assessment, portfolio assessment, personal conferences, peer reviews, laboratory logs or journals, videotape analysis, involving students in determining task criteria and rubrics, self-assessment activities for individual and group work.

Category B: Planning the Classroom Layout and Managing Routine Procedures

___ 1. My classroom has flexible seating so students can work together in pairs or small groups to work on projects or to conduct peer reviews.

___ 2. I have a place for storing student work in progress (model-making, collections, demonstrations, computer reports) while they are being assembled or graded.

___ 3. I use milk crates or file boxes to house folders containing student work in progress.

___ 4. I have a (relatively) private conferencing area where I can meet one-on-one with a student while others in the class complete individual or group work.

___ 5. I have a bulletin board or wall/counter surface where I can display samples of student work that exceed standards, meet most standards, do not meet standards.

___ 6. I have developed: (a) cover page summary forms to be completed by the student, (b) lists of task criteria for products and performances, (c) response journal writing prompts, (d) tentative scoring rubrics to rate products and performances, (e) student self-assessment forms for use with specific learning/assessment tasks. Each of these can be attached to actual work samples.

___ 7. I have established classroom procedures and routines to help save energy and maximize time on learning. These include: (a) posting a daily agenda, (b) distributing lists of individual and small group tasks, both required and optional, for my course, (c) using a signaling system to get everyone's attention, (d) posting classroom rules, (e) employing study buddies to help students who have missed classes, (f) devising collection systems for homework assignments and other learning products, (g) posting work group configurations and tasks.

Category C: Designing Learning Activities

___ 1. I have determined a key learning product or performance that will enable me to determine and document student proficiency for the essential skill and content areas of my subject during each marking period.

___ 2. The criteria I use to identify a good learning task include: (a) encourages students to ask questions and pursue answers, (b) has students learning to work independently and in teams, (c) has students practicing social and decision-making skills through presentations and demonstrations, (d) develops critical and creative thinking skills, (e) represents workplace roles and responsibilities.

___ 3. In planning daily lessons, I ask myself: (a) what opening strategy will I use to review, provide an overview, motivate, or tap into prior knowledge, (b) what new information will I provide, and how will students access it (lecture, demonstration, reading, computer search, videotape), (c) how will students have an opportunity to process, practice, or apply the new information during the class, (d) what learning products can students produce to demonstrate learning and accountability, (e) how can I best provide closure to the day's work? (summaries, report-outs, homework assignment)

___ 4. I have included activities in my lesson that allow for varied learning styles and multiple intelligences.

___ 5. I review my lesson plans with a critical eye on (a) pacing, (b) variety in materials and activities, (c) active student participation.

_____ 6. I build in transitional activities (activators, energizers, summarizers) to reinforce learning.

_____ 7. I incorporate alternative assessment tasks (portfolio, products, peer reviews, performance tasks, videotape analysis, journal entries) into my overall grading system for each marking period.

_____ 8. In designing units, I consider community resources (people, places, programs, policies, practices) that might be relevant to our curriculum.

_____ 9. I examine lesson content and available technology to determine if technology would be the best way to teach this content.

_____ 10. I work with our school library/media services to locate resources and schedule student research projects.

Category D: Launching New Instructional Approaches in My Classroom

_____ 1. I introduce the social skills I want students to practice during learning activities with their peers or with me such as scheduling a conference or extra help session, listening, checking for understanding, coming prepared with questions and materials, taking turns using equipment and materials, praising and challenging each other's thinking.

_____ 2. I give students opportunity to develop teamwork and collaboration skills using "practice" tasks in which they reflect on the things they did well individually and as a group.

_____ 3. I teach my students to use decision-making tools (weighted voting, criteria matrix, weighted pairs) and brainstorming procedures to improve their group work.

_____ 4. I provide a menu of choices for students to use in documenting or presenting their proficiency at certain tasks.

_____ 5. I encourage students to brainstorm areas for inquiry and ask them to suggest activities that might be appropriate as a means of pursuing answers to their own questions.

_____ 6. I demonstrate models of inquiry processes and problem-solving steps and tools.

_____ 7. I help students use a variety of research skills, resources, and materials in completing their investigations.

_____ 8. My assessment tasks require students to master and display skills that go beyond the accumulation of information.

_____ 9. I have written a letter to parents of my students explaining the purposes of new learning approaches in my class and how they will benefit students.

_____ 10. I meet with colleagues to compare experiences and to exchange successful strategies for organizing learning.

Category E: Evaluating the Impact of Block-Schedule Teaching and Learning

_____ 1. I keep a journal in which I record my thoughts and actions related to teaching in a block-scheduled classroom.

_____ 2. I ask my students what they think about the new approaches we are using in class.

_____ 3. I use data collected from students to improve learning tasks and classroom procedures.

_____ 4. I am learning things about my students that shorter learning segments would not reveal.

_____ 5. I am developing better personal relations with my students.

_____ 6. I am responding more to individual learning preferences and needs.

_____ 7. I am developing or using new curriculum materials and activities.

_____ 8. I am spending more time consulting with my colleagues.

_____ 9. My students are taking more responsibility for their own learning.

_____ 10. My students are learning to become effective self-assessors of their own work.

_____ 11. My students are becoming better organized in their work habits.

_____ 12. My students are demonstrating higher levels of thinking.

_____ 13. My students have more time to apply and practice the skills of my subject area.

_____ 14. My students are showing more seriousness of purpose.

_____ 15. Product- and performance-based assessments are helping me to identify what to reteach or reinforce.

_____ 16. Product- and performance-based assessments are enabling me to illustrate more effectively student learning progress to parents.

"ACTION STEPS FOR BLOCK SCHEDULING"

Sample Planning Worksheet

Category A: Background Reading and Preparation

Category B: Planning the Classroom Layout and Managing Routine Procedures

Category C: Designing Learning Activities

Category D: Launching New Instructional Approaches in My Classroom

APPENDIX B

CHECKLIST FOR MONITORING AND ASSESSING SMALL GROUP LEARNING

Decisions

- Determine size of group, based on nature of task, time available, experience of students, experience of teacher. _____

- Assign students to group. Indicate whether teacher-selected, student-selected, teacher- and student-selected, random, interest-based. _____

- Arrange room so team members can sit close enough together to communicate without disrupting other groups. _____

- Identify and collect instructional materials and resources to promote interdependence by distributing different supplies, assigning different portions of the lesson or different tasks, etc. _____

- Assign roles of facilitator, summarizer, recorder, timekeeper, etc., to ensure interdependence. _____

- Establish group norms such as trying, asking for help, offering help, being polite, encouraging each other, etc. _____

- Establish individual responsibilities such as quizzes. _____

- Establish group responsibilities such as a product or project. _____

Monitoring and Intervening

- Groups are formed quickly; students find their group location easily. _____

- Task is clearly described to students. _____

- Students demonstrate expected social skills such as listening, taking turns, sharing materials, paraphrasing, summarizing, encouraging, etc. _____

- Transitions are made quickly and smoothly. _____

- Signaling and similar devices (hand-in-air to signal for quiet, etc.) are used to speed work. _____

- Task assistance is provided. _____

- Student behavior is monitored. _____

- Intervention is provided to teach communication or social skills when needed. _____

- Closure is provided for lesson. _____

Evaluating and Processing

1. Assessment of task: _____
   - student self-assessment
   - group self-assessment
   - teacher observation/checklist

2. Assessment of group process (functioning): _____
   - student self-assessment
   - group self-assessment
   - teacher observation/checklist

3. Feedback to groups: _____
   - How well groups worked together
   - How groups can improve
   - Strategies for analysis, synthesis, and evaluation